OFFICIAL
NBA
TRIVIA

OFFICIAL NBA TRIVIA

CLARE MARTIN

HarperEntertainment
A Division of HarperCollinsPublishers

HarperEntertainment
A Division of HarperCollins*Publishers*
10 East 53rd Street, New York, NY 10022–5299

ISBN 0-06-107360-1

HarperCollins®, ®, and HarperEntertainment™ are trademarks of HarperCollins Publishers Inc.

First printing: October 1999

Printed in the United States of America

Visit HarperEntertainment on the World Wide Web at http://www.harpercollins.com

07 08 ❖/RRD 10

Contents

Introduction

by Clare Martin

It's tipoff time for *Official NBA Trivia,* a team-by-team challenge guaranteed to test even the most avid basketball fan. From the Blazers to the Bucks, from the Warriors to the Wizards, the teams, players, and history of the NBA have been translated into a series of questions and answers for the ultimate game of hoop trivia.

All of the NBA's twenty-nine franchises are represented here, each with its own chapter filled with interesting and unusual facts and statistics about the greatest legends that the National Basketball Association has ever seen. You can also quiz yourself on NBA basketball basics in the final chapter, "Rules of the Game."

Each chapter consists of twenty-five trivia questions designed to test your knowledge of more than fifty years of NBA action, from historical highlights to current champions. Start off with three free throw questions worth one point each as a warm up, then see how many of the two-pointers you can answer correctly before finishing with three difficult bonus questions, otherwise known as three-pointers, for a total of fifty points per chapter. Then see if your score is high enough for NBA Trivia All-Star honors.

So get ready to begin playing the trivia game of your life. It's Game Seven of the NBA Trivia Finals. The championship is on the line. Take your best shot and see if you can get in the zone—the NBA trivia zone.

OFFICIAL
NBA
TRIVIA

ATLANTA HAWKS

From the Tri-Cities to Atlanta, the Hawks have flown high with stars such as Bob Pettit, Dominique Wilkins, and Dikembe Mutombo. Even their coaches have been a stellar group of basketball strategists.

FREE THROWS

1. **Whose coaching record did Hawks coach Lenny Wilkens break when he won his 939th game?**
   - A. Bill Fitch
   - B. Red Auerbach
   - C. Dick Motta
   - D. Pat Riley

2. **Name the Hawks star who was known as the "Human Highlight Film."**
   - A. Gerald Wilkins
   - B. Dominique Wilkins
   - C. Freeman Williams
   - D. Spud Webb

3. **What NBA superstar went to the same college as Atlanta's Steve Smith?**
   A. Magic Johnson
   B. Isiah Thomas
   C. Michael Jordan
   D. Julius Erving

Two-Pointers

4. **Name the building where the Hawks played their home games until 1997–98.**
   A. Georgia Dome
   B. The Omni
   C. Atlanta Coliseum
   D. Alexander Memorial Coliseum

5. **Doc Rivers set a Hawks single-season record in which category with 823?**
   A. assists
   B. steals
   C. rebounds
   D. free throws made

6. **Which of the following players was *not* drafted by the Hawks?**
   A. Pete Maravich
   B. David Thompson
   C. Byron Scott
   D. Arvidas Sabonis

7. **Which Hawks player was the only four-time winner of the All-Star Game MVP award?**
   A. Lou Hudson
   B. Bob Pettit
   C. Dominique Wilkins
   D. Dikembe Mutombo

8. **Name the first Hawk ever to lead the NBA in scoring.**
   A. Kevin Willis
   B. Dominique Wilkins
   C. John Drew
   D. Bob Pettit

9. **Both Red Auerbach and Red Holzman served as coaches for the Hawks franchise. Which of the following coaches *never* guided the Hawks?**
   A. Del Harris
   B. Mike Fratello
   C. Hubie Brown
   D. Cotton Fitzsimmons

10. **Which Hawk became the shortest player to win the Slam-Dunk title at NBA All-Star Weekend?**
    A. Alan Henderson
    B. Steve Smith
    C. Spud Webb
    D. Ken Norman

11. **What is guard Mookie Blaylock's real first name?**
    A. Devon
    B. Darryl
    C. Darnell
    D. Daron

12. **Which Hawk led the league for three consecutive seasons in blocked shots per game?**
    A. Tree Rollins
    B. Kevin Willis
    C. Dikembe Mutombo
    D. Andrew Lang

13. **Which of the following players had his number 23 jersey retired by the Hawks?**
    A. Lou Hudson
    B. Bob Pettit
    C. Cliff Hagan
    D. John Drew

14. **Who is the Hawks' all-time leading scorer?**
    A. Bob Pettit
    B. Dominique Wilkins
    C. Lou Hudson
    D. Cliff Hagan

15. **Tree Rollins played 11 seasons for the Hawks. He went on to serve as an assistant coach with which NBA team?**
    A. Miami
    B. Charlotte
    C. Orlando
    D. Washington

16. **Name the former Hawk who was a member of the 1992 Men's Olympic Basketball Team.**
    A. Dominique Wilkins
    B. Steve Smith
    C. Christian Laettner
    D. Doc Rivers

17. **What is the most games that the Hawks have won in a single season?**
    A. 50
    B. 57
    C. 60
    D. 62

18. **Which of the following players did *not* attend the same college as Dikembe Mutombo?**
    A. Patrick Ewing
    B. Alonzo Mourning
    C. Othella Harrington
    D. Mark Jackson

19. **Which Hawk won the NBA Most Improved Player award in 1997–98?**
    A. Alan Henderson
    B. Steve Smith
    C. Christian Laettner
    D. Mookie Blaylock

20. **In the 1972–73 season, the Hawks had two players who scored more than 2,000 points. Who were they?**
    A. Pete Maravich and Walt Bellamy
    B. Lou Hudson and Herm Gilliam
    C. Pete Maravich and Lou Hudson
    D. Walt Bellamy and Herm Gilliam

21. **Name the Hawk who led the NBA in steals for the second consecutive season in 1997–98.**
    A. Steve Smith
    B. Mookie Blaylock
    C. Tyrone Corbin
    D. Alan Henderson

22. **Dominique Wilkins played for the Hawks for eleven and a half seasons, but he was traded to the L.A. Clippers in 1994. For which player was Dominique Wilkins traded?**
    A. Loy Vaught
    B. Ron Harper
    C. Charles Smith
    D. Danny Manning

BONUS THREE-POINTERS

23. Which Hawks coach won the inaugural NBA Coach of the Year award in 1962–63?
  A. Harry Gallatin
  B. Richie Guerin
  C. Alex Hannum
  D. Kevin Loughery

24. Name the team that the St. Louis Hawks beat in the 1958 Finals to win their first NBA title.
  A. Philadelphia
  B. Boston
  C. Milwaukee
  D. New York

25. Which of the following cities was not one of the Tri-Cities?
  A. Moline, Illinois
  B. Rock Island, Illinois
  C. Davenport, Iowa
  D. Des Moines, Iowa

◑ ANSWERS

1. B	14. B
2. B	15. C
3. A	16. C
4. B	17. B
5. A	18. D
6. C	19. A
7. B	20. C
8. D	21. B
9. A	22. D
10. C	23. A
11. D	24. B
12. C	25. D
13. A	

CHAPTER 2

BOSTON CELTICS

One of the NBA's original franchises, the Boston Celtics are one of sports' most successful teams of all time. One look at Boston's row of championship banners brings to mind some of basketball's greatest memories.

FREE THROWS

1. **The Celtics have won more NBA titles than any other franchise. How many banners does Boston have?**
   - A. 14
   - B. 16
   - C. 17
   - D. 18

2. **Which Celtic was nicknamed "Chief"?**
   - A. Robert Parish
   - B. Sam Jones
   - C. Wayne Embry
   - D. Don Chaney

3. **Who was the Celtics' first-round draft pick in 1996?**
   A. Ron Mercer
   B. Eric Williams
   C. Chauncey Billups
   D. Antoine Walker

TWO-POINTERS

4. **Which Celtic made the first three-pointer in NBA history?**
   A. Chris Ford
   B. Larry Bird
   C. Rick Robey
   D. Scott Wedman

5. **In which season did the Celtics compile the league's best-ever home record at 40–1?**
   A. 1973–74
   B. 1975–76
   C. 1980–81
   D. 1985–86

6. **Bill Russell has won more titles than anyone in NBA history. How many titles has Russell won?**
   A. 8
   B. 9
   C. 10
   D. 11

7. **In 1951, Boston hosted the first NBA All-Star Game. Which Celtic won the MVP award?**
   A. Bob Cousy
   B. Dick McGuire
   C. Ed Macauley
   D. Bill Sharman

8. How many times have the Celtics and the Lakers met in the NBA Finals?
   A. 7
   B. 8
   C. 10
   D. 12

9. During which season did the Celtics move from historic Boston Garden to the FleetCenter?
   A. 1993–94
   B. 1994–95
   C. 1995–96
   D. 1996–97

10. Against which team did the Celtics win the triple-overtime Finals thriller in 1976?
    A. Los Angeles Lakers
    B. Phoenix Suns
    C. Houston Rockets
    D. Golden State Warriors

11. How many times did Boston's Bob Cousy win the assists title?
    A. 5
    B. 6
    C. 7
    D. 8

12. Which team did Larry Bird and the Celtics beat in 1981 to capture the first of his three NBA championships?
    A. Houston Rockets
    B. Los Angeles Lakers
    C. Seattle SuperSonics
    D. Portland Trail Blazers

13. **Who took over as the Celtics coach after the retirement of Red Auerbach in 1966?**
    A. Bill Russell
    B. Tom Heinsohn
    C. Bill Fitch
    D. K.C. Jones

14. **True or false: No Celtic has ever led the league in scoring.**
    True
    False

15. **Against which team were the Celtics playing when broadcaster Johnny Most made the legendary call "Havlicek steals the ball!"?**
    A. Philadelphia
    B. New York
    C. Los Angeles Lakers
    D. St. Louis

16. **The Celtics have a long history of great sixth men. Name the most recent Celtic to win the NBA Sixth Man Award.**
    A. Kevin McHale
    B. Bill Walton
    C. John Havlicek
    D. Frank Ramsey

17. **Who was the first Celtic to win Rookie of the Year honors?**
    A. Tom Heinsohn
    B. Dave Cowens
    C. Bob Cousy
    D. Bill Russell

18. **Which Celtic was selected by the Cleveland Browns as a wide receiver in the 1962 NFL Draft?**
    A. Tom Sanders
    B. Mel Counts
    C. John Thompson
    D. John Havlicek

19. **How many consecutive NBA championships did Boston win?**
    A. 5
    B. 6
    C. 7
    D. 8

20. **Which Celtic went on to become president of the Lakers?**
    A. Jerry West
    B. Bill Sharman
    C. Mitch Kupchak
    D. Bennie Swain

21. **Which Celtic was the MVP of the 1976 NBA Finals?**
    A. Dave Cowens
    B. John Havlicek
    C. Jo Jo White
    D. Paul Silas

22. **With which team did Red Auerbach begin his pro coaching career?**
    A. Washington Capitols
    B. Boston Celtics
    C. Tri-Cities Blackhawks
    D. Rochester Royals

BONUS THREE-POINTERS

23. **Which Celtic went on to star in the TV series *The Rifleman*?**
    A. Virgil Vaughn
    B. Chuck Cooper
    C. Chuck Connors
    D. Willie Naulls

24. **Even though the Celtics have moved from the Boston Garden to the FleetCenter, they still play on the same parquet floor that they played on at the Garden. How many wood panels make up that famous floor?**
    A. 179
    B. 247
    C. 343
    D. 451

25. **Larry Bird made the number 33 famous in Boston, but which Celtic wore that number just prior to Bird?**
    A. Steve Kuberski
    B. Jim Ard
    C. Henry Finkel
    D. Ed Searcy

● ANSWERS

1. B	10. B	19. D
2. A	11. D	20. B
3. D	12. A	21. C
4. A	13. A	22. A
5. D	14. True	23. C
6. D	15. A	24. B
7. C	16. B	25. A
8. C	17. A	
9. C	18. D	

CHAPTER 3

CHARLOTTE HORNETS

Since joining the NBA for the 1988–89 season, the Charlotte Hornets have won a place in the hearts of the many basketball fans in North Carolina. The hard-working Hornets have done their best to carry on the state's well-known tradition of excellence in the game of basketball.

FREE THROWS

1. **What is the nickname of Charlotte Coliseum?**
   A. Buzz Central
   B. Hornet House
   C. The Hive
   D. The Bees' Nest

2. **Name the first coach of the Hornets.**
   A. Dick Harter
   B. Gene Littles
   C. Allan Bristow
   D. Dave Cowens

3. **What is the name of the Hornets' mascot?**
   A. Harvey
   B. Hugo
   C. Harold
   D. Humphrey

Two-Pointers

4. **Which Hornet was the winner of the 1994 NBA Sixth Man Award?**
   A. Anthony Mason
   B. Kenny Gattison
   C. Dell Curry
   D. Eddie Johnson

5. **The Hornets made their first playoff appearance in 1992–93. Who was their first-round opponent?**
   A. New York
   B. Boston
   C. Chicago
   D. Atlanta

6. **As a college senior, this player was named MVP of the Southwest Conference.**
   A. Bobby Phills
   B. David Wesley
   C. Elden Campbell
   D. Eddie Jones

7. **In October 1994, the Hornets traveled to Paris to play a preseason game against which NBA team?**
   A. Seattle
   B. Houston
   C. Golden State
   D. Indiana

8. **This NBA veteran was playing for Charlotte when he set a career record for NBA games played.**
   A. Kelly Tripucka
   B. Mike Gminski
   C. Kurt Rambis
   D. Robert Parish

9. **Which Hornet set NBA All-Star records for points in a half (24) and points in a quarter (20)?**
   A. Larry Johnson
   B. Alonzo Mourning
   C. Glen Rice
   D. Eddie Jones

10. **Who was the first player ever selected by the Hornets in the NBA Draft?**
    A. Tom Tolbert
    B. Rex Chapman
    C. Jeff Moore
    D. J.R. Reid

11. **Which of the NBA's yearly awards was won by Larry Johnson when he played for Charlotte?**
    A. Rookie of the Year
    B. Sixth Man award
    C. Defensive Player of the Year
    D. J. Walter Kennedy Citizenship award

12. **Which Hornet left Syracuse as the school's all-time leading scorer?**
    A. LeRon Ellis
    B. Derrick Coleman
    C. Hersey Hawkins
    D. Eddie Johnson

13. Name the Hornet who scored 48 points against the Celtics on March 6, 1997.
    A. Kenny Anderson
    B. Michael Adams
    C. Glen Rice
    D. Anthony Mason

14. Who is Charlotte's career leader in blocked shots?
    A. Alonzo Mourning
    B. Kenny Gattison
    C. Vlade Divac
    D. Matt Geiger

15. Who led the Hornets in steals for the team's first five seasons?
    A. Dell Curry
    B. Kendall Gill
    C. Muggsy Bogues
    D. Hersey Hawkins

16. Name the first Hornet to appear in an NBA All-Star Game.
    A. Glen Rice
    B. Alonzo Mourning
    C. Larry Johnson
    D. Dell Curry

17. For many years there was a minor league baseball team in Charlotte called the Hornets. With which major league team were they affiliated?
    A. Atlanta Braves
    B. Minnesota Twins
    C. Texas Rangers
    D. Pittsburgh Pirates

18. **In which country did Anthony Mason play professionally in 1988–89?**
    A. Greece
    B. Turkey
    C. Australia
    D. Israel

19. **This player was named MVP of the Rookie Game at the 1995 NBA All-Star Weekend.**
    A. George Zidek
    B. Scott Burrell
    C. Eddie Jones
    D. Tony Delk

20. **Who ranks as the Charlotte Hornets' all-time leading scorer?**
    A. Dell Curry
    B. Rex Chapman
    C. Muggsy Bogues
    D. Glen Rice

21. **What was the original nickname of Charlotte's NBA franchise before it became the Hornets?**
    A. Stingers
    B. Barons
    C. Pride
    D. Spirit

22. **As a college senior at Southern, Bobby Phills led the nation in this category.**
    A. three-pointers per game
    B. free throw percentage
    C. steals per game
    D. assists per game

BONUS THREE-POINTERS

23. Who scored the first points for Charlotte in the Hornets' first game?

A. Rex Chapman
B. Robert Reid
C. Kelly Tripucka
D. Tim Kempton

24. Which of the following players never recorded a triple-double as a Hornet?

A. Larry Johnson
B. Kendall Gill
C. Anthony Mason
D. Glen Rice

25. Charlotte led the NBA in attendance for seven straight seasons before being dethroned by which team in 1997–98?

A. Toronto
B. Portland
C. Chicago
D. Minnesota

● ANSWERS

I. C	10. B	19. C
2. A	11. A	20. A
3. B	12. B	21. D
4. C	13. C	22. A
5. B	14. A	23. C
6. B	15. C	24. D
7. C	16. C	25. C
8. D	17. B	
9. C	18. B	

CHICAGO BULLS

The Chicago Bulls have proven that good things do come to those who wait. It wasn't until the 1990s that the team developed into one of the best in NBA history, winning six titles in eight years, showcasing a superstar named Michael Jordan and creating a legacy that will never be forgotten.

FREE THROWS

1. **What jersey number was worn by Michael Jordan?**
    A. 17
    B. 23
    C. 33
    D. 34

2. **Which former Chicago star went on to coach the Utah Jazz?**
    A. Norm Van Lier
    B. Mickey Johnson
    C. Jerry Sloan
    D. Gene Banks

3. **Name the well-known Bulls broadcaster who was also the first coach of the team in 1966.**
   A. Johnny Kerr
   B. Chick Hearn
   C. Ray Clay
   D. Dick Motta

TWO-POINTERS

4. **How many games did the Chicago Bulls win during the 1995–96 season to set an NBA record for games won in a single season?**
   A. 65
   B. 69
   C. 72
   D. 80

5. **Ron Harper's collegiate jersey number 9 is the only one ever retired by this college.**
   A. Ohio State
   B. Miami
   C. Miami of Ohio
   D. Ohio Wesleyan

6. **Which of the following teams have the Bulls never beaten in the NBA Finals?**
   A. Portland
   B. Seattle
   C. Phoenix
   D. Houston

7. **Which Bull led the team in scoring in 1993–94 and 1994–95?**
   A. Michael Jordan
   B. Scottie Pippen
   C. Toni Kukoc
   D. B.J. Armstrong

8. **Which player holds the Bulls' career record for field goal percentage?**
   A. Gene Banks
   B. Artis Gilmore
   C. Orlando Woolridge
   D. Horace Grant

9. **Name the only player in Bulls' history to have a quadruple-double.**
   A. Jerry Sloan
   B. Michael Jordan
   C. Nate Thurmond
   D. Scottie Pippen

10. **Michael Jordan was MVP of the NBA All-Star Game three times. Who is the only other Bull to win All-Star MVP honors?**
    A. Reggie Theus
    B. Scottie Pippen
    C. Bob Love
    D. Artis Gilmore

11. **Which Bull led the league in three-point field goal percentage in 1992–93?**
    A. Steve Kerr
    B. Michael Jordan
    C. Scottie Pippen
    D. B.J. Armstrong

12. **Which of the following players never led the Bulls in rebounding for a season?**
    A. Artis Gilmore
    B. Luc Longley
    C. Tom Boerwinkle
    D. David Greenwood

13. Phil Jackson and Johnny Kerr both won Coach of the Year honors with Chicago. Which other Bulls coach also won that award?
    A. Dick Motta
    B. Kevin Loughery
    C. Jerry Sloan
    D. Doug Collins

14. Against which team did Michael Jordan score his career-high 69 points?
    A. New York
    B. Portland
    C. Cleveland
    D. Charlotte

15. Whose draft rights were traded to Seattle in exchange for the draft rights to Scottie Pippen?
    A. Shawn Kemp
    B. Hersey Hawkins
    C. Olden Polynice
    D. Gary Payton

16. Chicago set an NBA Finals record for largest margin of victory in a game against which team?
    A. Seattle SuperSonics
    B. Los Angeles Lakers
    C. Portland Trail Blazers
    D. Utah Jazz

17. Which Chicago player won the AT&T Shootout at the NBA All-Star Weekend three times?
    A. Craig Hodges
    B. B.J. Armstrong
    C. Steve Kerr
    D. Reggie Theus

18. **Which of the following awards did Michael Jordan never win?**
    A. Defensive Player of the Year
    B. Most Improved Player
    C. Rookie of the Year
    D. Most Valuable Player

19. **How many times did Toni Kukoc win the European Player of the Year award?**
    A. 1
    B. 2
    C. 3
    D. 4

20. **This Bulls assistant has been a coach at the collegiate Division I or professional level for more than 50 years.**
    A. Tex Winter
    B. Frank Hamblen
    C. Jim Cleamons
    D. Johnny Bach

21. **Who was the Bulls' head coach in Michael Jordan's first season with the team?**
    A. Kevin Loughery
    B. Stan Albeck
    C. Rod Thorn
    D. Doug Collins

22. **In whose honor was jersey number 10 retired by the Chicago Bulls?**
    A. Jerry Sloan
    B. Gene Banks
    C. Artis Gilmore
    D. Bob Love

BONUS THREE-POINTERS

23. Before the Bulls joined the NBA, there was another NBA team in Chicago. What was that team's nickname?

    A. Jets
    B. Stags
    C. Rebels
    D. Steamrollers

24. Name the Bull who holds the franchise record for most consecutive free throws made (49).

    A. Craig Hodges
    B. Chet Walker
    C. Ricky Sobers
    D. Sam Vincent

25. Who was the first Chicago player to record a triple-double?

    A. Clifford Ray
    B. Clem Haskins
    C. Guy Rodgers
    D. Norm Van Lier

🎾 ANSWERS

1. B		14. C	
2. C		15. C	
3. A		16. D	
4. C		17. A	
5. C		18. B	
6. D		19. C	
7. B		20. A	
8. B		21. A	
9. C		22. D	
10. B		23. B	
11. D		24. C	
12. B		25. C	
13. A			

CLEVELAND CAVALIERS

The Cleveland Cavaliers always present a challenge in the Central Division. From Austin Carr to Larry Nance to Mark Price and Brad Daugherty, the history of the team has been intertwined with players whose hard work and dedication to the game will always be admired.

FREE THROWS

1. **Cleveland head coach Mike Fratello spent seven seasons coaching which other Central Division team?**
   A. Indiana
   B. Atlanta
   C. Milwaukee
   D. Chicago

2. **Which Cavalier was a two-time winner of the Long Distance Shootout at NBA All-Star Weekend?**
   A. Steve Kerr
   B. Mark Price
   C. Dan Majerle
   D. Craig Ehlo

3. **Cleveland's Shawn Kemp grew up in which state?**
    A. New York
    B. Kentucky
    C. California
    D. Indiana

TWO-POINTERS

4. **Which Cavalier was the first player in ACC history to accumulate at least 2,000 career points, 1,000 rebounds, and 500 assists?**
    A. Danny Ferry
    B. Chucky Brown
    C. Brad Daugherty
    D. Larry Nance

5. **Through 1998, Cleveland had selected only two players with the first overall pick in the NBA Draft. One was Brad Daugherty. Name the other.**
    A. Charles Oakley
    B. Kevin Johnson
    C. Austin Carr
    D. Terrell Brandon

6. **Which of the following coaches has never coached the Cavaliers?**
    A. George Karl
    B. Chuck Daly
    C. Bill Fitch
    D. Kevin Loughery

7. **This Hall of Famer finished his career in Cleveland after starring for many years with the Warriors.**
    A. Rick Barry
    B. Jamaal Wilkes
    C. Nate Thurmond
    D. Cazzie Russell

8. **Who is Cleveland's all-time leader in assists?**
   A. John Bagley
   B. Foots Walker
   C. Terrell Brandon
   D. Mark Price

9. **Which Cavalier won the Francis Pomeroy Naismith award for the best college player under 6 feet?**
   A. Austin Carr
   B. Brevin Knight
   C. Jim Cleamons
   D. Kevin Johnson

10. **In which home arena did the Cavaliers play during their inaugural season?**
    A. Cleveland Arena
    B. Gund Arena
    C. Richfield Coliseum
    D. Cleveland Civic Center

11. **This Cavalier rookie won MVP honors at the Rookie Game at the 1998 NBA All-Star Weekend.**
    A. Brevin Knight
    B. Zydrunas Ilgauskas
    C. Derek Anderson
    D. Vitaly Potapenko

12. **Which of the following players never played for Cleveland?**
    A. Bill Laimbeer
    B. Walt Frazier
    C. Fred Roberts
    D. Bob Dandridge

13. **Which U.S. college did Ukrainian Vitaly Potapenko attend?**
    A. Wright State
    B. Marquette
    C. Southern
    D. Xavier

14. **This Cleveland player was a member of the 1996 NCAA Division I championship team.**
    A. Antonio Lang
    B. Brevin Knight
    C. Derek Anderson
    D. Mitchell Butler

15. **Mark Price holds the NBA career record for highest free throw percentage at what number?**
    A. .904
    B. .909
    C. .914
    D. .921

16. **This Cavalier became the first player since Charles Barkley to switch conferences and be named an All-Star starter in each conference.**
    A. Mark Price
    B. Shawn Kemp
    C. Kevin Johnson
    D. Larry Nance

17. **In 1972, Seattle's Lenny Wilkens was traded with Barry Clemens to Cleveland for which player?**
    A. Jim Cleamons
    B. Cornell Warner
    C. Butch Beard
    D. Rick Roberson

18. When the 1998–99 season began, only one player in Cleveland history had scored 50 or more points in a game. Name him.
    A. World B. Free
    B. Mike Mitchell
    C. Brad Daugherty
    D. Walt Wesley

19. Which Cleveland player once collected a franchise-high 27 assists against Golden State?
    A. Geoff Huston
    B. Mark Price
    C. Lenny Wilkens
    D. Brevin Knight

20. Wesley Person is the third-leading scorer in Auburn history, trailing only his brother Chuck and which former Cavalier?
    A. Elmore Smith
    B. Jim Brewer
    C. Mike Mitchell
    D. Derrick Chievous

21. Which Cleveland coach won Coach of the Year honors in 1975–76?
    A. Bill Fitch
    B. Stan Albeck
    C. Tom Nisalke
    D. Lenny Wilkens

22. Which of the following players has not had his jersey number retired by the Cavaliers?
    A. Bingo Smith
    B. Larry Nance
    C. Campy Russell
    D. Austin Carr

BONUS THREE-POINTERS

23. **After being selected by Cleveland in the Expansion Draft, this player spent the Cavs' first season in the army instead of on the court.**
    A. John Johnson
    B. Butch Beard
    C. John Warren
    D. Steve Patterson

24. **Throughout the 1998–99 season, who was the Cavs' all-time leader in games played?**
    A. Danny Ferry
    B. Austin Carr
    C. Bingo Smith
    D. John Williams

25. **"Foots" Walker led the Cavaliers in steals for three seasons. What was his first name?**
    A. Calvin
    B. Calvert
    C. Clark
    D. Clarence

🎾 ANSWERS

1. B	10. A	19. A
2. B	11. B	20. C
3. D	12. D	21. A
4. A	13. A	22. C
5. C	14. C	23. B
6. D	15. A	24. C
7. C	16. B	25. D
8. D	17. C	
9. B	18. D	

DALLAS
MAVERICKS

DALLAS MAVERICKS

The Dallas Mavericks joined the league in 1980, and as the team finishes its second decade, the Mavericks are once again an up-and-coming team. NBA opponents have learned the hard way not to take these Mavs lightly.

FREE THROWS

1. **Which country does Chris Anstey call home?**
   A. England
   B. Australia
   C. Canada
   D. New Zealand

2. **A new arena is under construction, but in which building have the Mavericks played their home games since joining the league?**
   A. Reunion Arena
   B. ARCO Arena
   C. Bradley Center
   D. Target Center

3. **What is Hot Rod Williams's first name?**
   A. Rodney
   B. Roderick
   C. John
   D. James

Two-Pointers

4. **Name the Mavericks' career leader in points.**
   A. Mark Aguirre
   B. Derek Harper
   C. Brad Davis
   D. Rolando Blackman

5. **Which Maverick won the 1988 NBA Sixth Man award?**
   A. James Donaldson
   B. Roy Tarpley
   C. Sam Perkins
   D. Bill Wennington

6. **Name the first Dallas player ever to lead the league in blocked shots.**
   A. Kurt Thomas
   B. Herb Williams
   C. Doug Smith
   D. Shawn Bradley

7. **Which of the following coaches had the longest tenure with the Mavericks?**
   A. Dick Motta
   B. John MacLeod
   C. Richie Adubato
   D. Don Nelson

8. On March 5, 1996, Dallas's George McCloud equaled an NBA record for most three-pointers attempted in a game with how many?
   A. 15
   B. 18
   C. 20
   D. 24

9. Name the Maverick who set a Dallas rookie record for points scored with 1,732.
   A. Jim Jackson
   B. Jay Vincent
   C. Jamal Mashburn
   D. James Donaldson

10. Which Maverick scored 50 points against Chicago on November 12, 1994?
    A. Jason Kidd
    B. George McCloud
    C. Roy Tarpley
    D. Jamal Mashburn

11. Two Mavericks have played in all 48 of Dallas's playoff games. One is Rolando Blackman. Name the other.
    A. Derek Harper
    B. Brad Davis
    C. Sam Perkins
    D. James Donaldson

12. Through 1998, who was the only player selected by Dallas with the first overall pick in the NBA Draft?
    A. Jamal Mashburn
    B. Jason Kidd
    C. Mark Aguirre
    D. Adrian Dantley

13. **Michael Finley is only the fourth Maverick to dish out more than 400 assists in a season. Which of the following Dallas players did not achieve this feat?**
    A. Brad Davis
    B. Derek Harper
    C. Jay Vincent
    D. Jason Kidd

14. **Hubert Davis is the nephew of which other NBA player?**
    A. Johnny Davis
    B. Warren Davis
    C. Terry Davis
    D. Walter Davis

15. **Which Maverick holds the franchise record for most consecutive games played with 246?**
    A. Derek Harper
    B. Brad Davis
    C. Rolando Blackman
    D. Herb Williams

16. **He was a co-winner of the NBA Rookie of the Year award as a player with Dallas.**
    A. Jamal Mashburn
    B. Jason Kidd
    C. Jim Jackson
    D. Michael Finley

17. **Which number was retired at Boston Garden in honor of Dallas coach Don Nelson's playing career with the Celtics?**
    A. 7
    B. 15
    C. 19
    D. 21

18. **Which Dallas player was traded to Phoenix in exchange for Cedric Ceballos?**
    - A. Jim Jackson
    - B. Jason Kidd
    - C. Dennis Scott
    - D. George McCloud

19. **With which NBA team did Rolando Blackman finish his professional career?**
    - A. New York
    - B. New Jersey
    - C. Golden State
    - D. Houston

20. **Which of the following players was not a first-round draft pick by the Mavericks?**
    - A. Detlef Schrempf
    - B. Sam Perkins
    - C. Kiki Vandeweghe
    - D. Ron Harper

21. **Name the Maverick who led the league in minutes played in 1997–98.**
    - A. A.C. Green
    - B. Robert Pack
    - C. Michael Finley
    - D. Khalid Reeves

22. **Whose jersey number 15 has been retired by the Mavericks?**
    - A. Rolando Blackman
    - B. Brad Davis
    - C. Derek Harper
    - D. Jay Vincent

BONUS THREE-POINTERS

23. Who collected the Mavericks' first-ever triple-double?
- A. Mark Aguirre
- B. Derek Harper
- C. Jason Kidd
- D. Michael Finley

24. Which player played in the most games for Dallas without starting?
- A. Steve Alford
- B. Sam Cassell
- C. Tony Dumas
- D. Fat Lever

25. What is the most frequently worn jersey number in Mavericks history?
- A. 17
- B. 20
- C. 21
- D. 24

🏀**ANSWERS**

I. B	14. D
2. A	15. B
3. C	16. B
4. D	17. C
5. B	18. C
6. D	19. A
7. A	20. D
8. C	21. C
9. B	22. B
10. D	23. A
11. A	24. A

DENVER NUGGETS

The Denver Nuggets have been a fixture in the Mile High City for years, beginning as an ABA franchise. These days, the young and talented Nuggets have made Denver a difficult destination on the NBA map.

FREE THROWS

1. **Whose nickname is "The Horse"?**
   - A. Reggie Williams
   - B. Dan Issel
   - C. Dan Schayes
   - D. Calvin Natt

2. **What is the name of the Nuggets' mascot?**
   - A. Boomer
   - B. Hugo
   - C. Rocky
   - D. Mountain Man

3. **Who coached the Nuggets for a franchise-high nine-plus seasons?**
   A. Doug Moe
   B. Larry Brown
   C. Bob Bass
   D. Alex Hannum

TWO-POINTERS

4. **What was Denver's nickname before the team became the Nuggets in 1974?**
   A. Diggers
   B. Rockets
   C. Bearcats
   D. Spirits

5. **Which Nugget won the 1993 NBA Most Improved Player award?**
   A. LaPhonso Ellis
   B. Todd Lichti
   C. Robert Pack
   D. Mahmoud Abdul-Rauf

6. **By which team was Antonio McDyess originally drafted?**
   A. Phoenix Suns
   B. Los Angeles Clippers
   C. Denver Nuggets
   D. New Jersey Nets

7. **Who was the only Denver player to win ABA MVP honors?**
   A. Spencer Hayward
   B. Bobby Jones
   C. David Thompson
   D. Mack Calvin

8. Before coming to Denver, Mike D'Antonio was one of the most successful coaches in the Italian Professional Basketball League. Which team did he guide to the championship in 1997?
   A. Scavolini Pesaro
   B. Benetton Treviso
   C. Philips Milan
   D. Kinder Bologna

9. Name the Nugget who led the league in scoring in 1982–83.
   A. David Thompson
   B. Fats Lever
   C. Kiki Vandeweghe
   D. Alex English

10. Which player set a Nuggets rookie record for free throw percentage with .832 in 1992–93?
    A. Mahmoud Abdul-Rauf
    B. LaPhonso Ellis
    C. Bryant Stith
    D. Dikembe Mutombo

11. Which team beat the Nuggets in their only trip to the ABA Finals in 1976?
    A. New York
    B. Indiana
    C. Kentucky
    D. San Antonio

12. Alex English ranks second in NBA history with eight consecutive seasons of 2,000 or more points. Who ranks first?
    A. Dominique Wilkins
    B. Karl Malone
    C. Michael Jordan
    D. Wilt Chamberlain

13. **Nick Van Exel came to the Nuggets in exchange for Tony Battie and the draft rights to which player?**
    A. Tremaine Fowlkes
    B. Ryan Bowen
    C. Tyronn Lue
    D. Brian Skinner

14. **Which Nugget was the MVP of the 1979 NBA All-Star Game?**
    A. David Thompson
    B. Mack Calvin
    C. Dan Issel
    D. George McGinnis

15. **Which Denver coach won NBA Coach of the Year honors in 1987–88?**
    A. Doug Moe
    B. Larry Brown
    C. Del Harris
    D. Donnie Walsh

16. **In 1996, Dikembe Mutombo collected 31 rebounds in a game against Charlotte, tying the Nuggets' record set by which player?**
    A. T.R. Dunn
    B. Ervin Johnson
    C. Jerome Lane
    D. Spencer Haywood

17. **In 1994, Denver became the first eighth seed ever to beat a top seed in the NBA Playoffs. Which team lost to the Nuggets?**
    A. Los Angeles Lakers
    B. Portland Trail Blazers
    C. Houston Rockets
    D. Seattle SuperSonics

18. **Which Nugget twice led the league in free throw percentage?**
    A. Michael Adams
    B. Mahmoud Abdul-Rauf
    C. Walter Davis
    D. Kiki Vandeweghe

19. **Which future Denver player was a member of the 1980 Olympic basketball team?**
    A. Bill Hanzlik
    B. Walter Davis
    C. Tom LaGarde
    D. Alex English

20. **In 1983, Denver played in the highest scoring game in NBA history, losing 186–184 in triple OT to which team?**
    A. Dallas
    B. Golden State
    C. Detroit
    D. Milwaukee

21. **Who is the Nuggets' all-time career leader in steals?**
    A. Fats Lever
    B. T.R. Dunn
    C. Alex English
    D. Bobby Jones

22. **David Thompson set a Nuggets scoring record by equaling the second-highest single-game point total in NBA history (no OT). How many points did he score?**
    A. 65
    B. 68
    C. 73
    D. 78

BONUS THREE-POINTERS

23. Name the player who was the first to be signed by the Denver franchise and the first to have his number retired.
    A. Dan Issell
    B. Byron Beck
    C. George Irvine
    D. Fatty Taylor

24. McNichols Sports Arena was the site of the first-ever slam-dunk contest held at the ABA All-Star Game in which year?
    A. 1973
    B. 1975
    C. 1976
    D. 1978

25. Twice in the '80s, the same two Nuggets scored more than 2,000 points in a single season. One was Alex English. Name the other.
    A. Kiki Vandeweghe
    B. Michael Adams
    C. Walter Davis
    D. Dan Issel

● ANSWERS

1. B	10. C	19. A
2. C	11. A	20. C
3. A	12. B	21. A
4. B	13. C	22. C
5. D	14. A	23. B
6. B	15. A	24. C
7. A	16. D	25. A
8. B	17. D	
9. D	18. B	

DETROIT PISTONS

Like the city they represent, the Detroit Pistons have always been known for their work ethic. From Dave Bing to Isiah Thomas to Grant Hill, Detroit has showcased some of the league's best athletes and leaders.

FREE THROWS

1. **Where did the Pistons play their home games immediately before moving to the Palace of Auburn Hills?**
    A. Joe Louis Arena
    B. Pontiac Silverdome
    C. Cobo Arena
    D. The Olympia

2. **What well-known college basketball announcer was once head coach of the Pistons?**
    A. Digger Phelps
    B. Dick Vitale
    C. Billy Packer
    D. Al McGuire

3. **Which Piston won back-to-back Defensive Player of the Year awards?**
   A. Dave Bing
   B. Bob Lanier
   C. Dennis Rodman
   D. Grant Hill

Two-Pointers

4. **Where was the Pistons' franchise located before moving to Detroit?**
   A. Lansing, Michigan
   B. Fort Wayne, Indiana
   C. Springfield, Illinois
   D. Rochester, New York

5. **Who was the MVP of the 1989 NBA Finals?**
   A. Joe Dumars
   B. Isiah Thomas
   C. Vinnie Johnson
   D. Dennis Rodman

6. **In 1989, the Pistons acquired Mark Aguirre from Dallas in exchange for which player?**
   A. James Edwards
   B. John Salley
   C. Adrian Dantley
   D. Rick Mahorn

7. **Which Piston was nicknamed "Spider"?**
   A. John Salley
   B. Kelly Tripucka
   C. George Yardley
   D. Bailey Howell

8. **Who was Isiah Thomas's college coach?**
   - A. John Thompson
   - B. Dean Smith
   - C. Bobby Knight
   - D. Ray Meyer

9. **In 1990, the Pistons became only the third franchise ever to win two consecutive NBA titles. Name the first two teams that accomplished the feat.**
   - A. Celtics and Sixers
   - B. Lakers and Sixers
   - C. Celtics and Lakers
   - D. Celtics and Trail Blazers

10. **Who is the Pistons' all-time leader in rebounds?**
    - A. Bill Laimbeer
    - B. Bob Lanier
    - C. Dennis Rodman
    - D. Walter Dukes

11. **Which of the following Pistons is *not* In the Hall of Fame?**
    - A. Bob Lanier
    - B. Dave Bing
    - C. Adrian Dantley
    - D. Bailey Howell

12. **In 1995, Grant Hill shared the Rookie of the Year award with which other player?**
    - A. Jason Kidd
    - B. Juwan Howard
    - C. Glenn Robinson
    - D. Eddie Jones

13. In one of the most frantic finishes in playoff history, Boston's Larry Bird stole the ball from a Piston and fed Dennis Johnson for the game-winning layup in Game 5 of the 1987 Eastern Conference Finals. Whose pass did Bird steal?
    A. Dennis Rodman
    B. Bill Laimbeer
    C. James Edwards
    D. Isiah Thomas

14. Which Piston was known as "The Microwave"?
    A. John Long
    B. Kent Benson
    C. Terry Dischinger
    D. Vinnie Johnson

15. Which Piston was twice named MVP of the NBA All-Star Game?
    A. Bailey Howell
    B. Bob Lanier
    C. Dave Bing
    D. Isiah Thomas

16. How many NCAA Championships did Detroit's Grant Hill win at Duke?
    A. 1
    B. 2
    C. 3
    D. 4

17. Which Detroit head coach was the youngest in NBA history? He was 24 years old at the time.
    A. Dave DeBusschere
    B. Ron Rothstein
    C. Red Rocha
    D. Ray Scott

18. On January 29, 1988, the Pistons set what was then an NBA regular-season attendance record with a crowd of 61,983. Who was Detroit's opponent?
    A. Boston Celtics
    B. Los Angeles Lakers
    C. Chicago Bulls
    D. Philadelphia 76ers

19. Where was Chuck Daly's next coaching job after leaving the Pistons?
    A. Orlando
    B. New Jersey
    C. Atlanta
    D. Charlotte

20. Which two former Pistons were college teammates at Notre Dame?
    A. Bill Laimbeer and Kelly Tripucka
    B. Kelly Tripucka and Adrian Dantley
    C. Adrian Dantley and Bill Laimbeer
    D. LaPhonso Ellis and Gary Brokaw

21. Which of the following Pistons was not Rookie of the Year?
    A. Dave Bing
    B. Grant Hill
    C. Don Meineke
    D. Isiah Thomas

22. Who was the Pistons' first-round draft pick in the 1998 NBA Draft?
    A. Bonzi Wells
    B. Korleone Young
    C. Scot Pollard
    D. Charles O'Bannon

BONUS THREE-POINTERS

23. **Denver's David Thompson was the MVP of the All-Star Game the last time it was played in Detroit. What year was that?**
    A. 1978
    B. 1979
    C. 1980
    D. 1981

24. **Which Piston led the NBA in scoring at 27.1 points per game in 1967–68?**
    A. Dave Bing
    B. Dave DeBusschere
    C. Eddie Miles
    D. Bob Lanier

25. **Name the former NBA referee who became coach of the Pistons.**
    A. Charles Wolf
    B. Charles Eckman
    C. Donnis Butcher
    D. Earl Lloyd

● ANSWERS

1. B	10. A	19. B
2. B	11. C	20. A
3. C	12. A	21. D
4. B	13. D	22. A
5. A	14. D	23. B
6. C	15. D	24. A
7. A	16. B	25. B
8. C	17. A	
9. C	18. A	

GOLDEN STATE WARRIORS

One of the NBA's original franchises, the Golden State Warriors have seen the league grow and prosper since 1946. Through the years, the Warriors' uniform has been worn by many greats of the game, from Wilt Chamberlain to Rick Barry to Chris Mullin.

FREE THROWS

1. **Which team did Warriors coach P.J. Carlesimo lead to the 1989 NCAA Final Four?**
   - A. St. John's
   - B. Seton Hall
   - C. Syracuse
   - D. Providence

2. **In which city were the Warriors first located?**
   - A. San Francisco
   - B. San Diego
   - C. Philadelphia
   - D. Pittsburgh

3. **How many points did Wilt Chamberlain score to set the NBA single-game record?**
   A. 75
   B. 87
   C. 93
   D. 100

Two-Pointers

4. **On which island did Adonal Foyle grow up?**
   A. Bahamas
   B. Canouan
   C. St. Croix
   D. Puerto Rico

5. **What was the nickname once given to the trio of Tim Hardaway, Mitch Richmond, and Chris Mullin?**
   A. Run TMC
   B. Three of a Kind
   C. Terrific Trio
   D. Golden Boys

6. **Prior to Joe Smith in 1995, name the last player the Warriors selected with the first overall pick in the NBA Draft.**
   A. Robert Parish
   B. Anfernee Hardaway
   C. Chris Mullin
   D. Joe Barry Carroll

7. **This Warrior led the NBA in steals in 1974–75.**
   A. Eric Floyd
   B. Rick Barry
   C. Purvis Short
   D. Sonny Parker

8. **Which of the following Warriors was not the NBA Rookie of the Year?**
   A. Keith Wilkes
   B. Woody Sauldsberry
   C. Mitch Richmond
   D. Chris Mullin

9. **Which team did the Warriors sweep in the 1975 NBA Finals?**
   A. Washington
   B. Philadelphia
   C. Boston
   D. New York

10. **Name the Warriors' all-time leading rebounder.**
    A. Wilt Chamberlain
    B. Nate Thurmond
    C. Larry Smith
    D. Paul Arizin

11. **Which year did John Starks win the NBA Sixth Man award?**
    A. 1995
    B. 1996
    C. 1997
    D. 1998

12. **Don Nelson won Coach of the Year honors for the Warriors in 1991–92. Which other Warriors coach won that award?**
    A. Bill Sharman
    B. Alex Hannum
    C. Al Attles
    D. George Senesky

13. **How many NBA titles did the Warriors win before moving to the Bay Area?**
    A. 1
    B. 2
    C. 3
    D. 4

14. **In which statistical category did Manute Bol lead the NBA in 1988–89?**
    A. blocked shots
    B. rebounds
    C. field goal percentage
    D. free throw percentage

15. **The Warriors are one of only three charter members of the NBA still playing, joining the Boston Celtics and which other team?**
    A. New York
    B. Chicago
    C. Detroit
    D. Milwaukee

16. **Which season did Wilt Chamberlain win both Rookie of the Year and MVP honors?**
    A. 1957–58
    B. 1959–60
    C. 1962–63
    D. 1963–64

17. **Donyell Marshall was acquired from Minnesota in exchange for which player?**
    A. Jerome Kersey
    B. Chris Mullin
    C. Tom Gugliotta
    D. B.J. Armstrong

18. Which of the following players has not had his jersey number retired by the Warriors?
    A. Wilt Chamberlain
    B. Al Attles
    C. Tom Meschery
    D. Nate Thurmond

19. By which team was Antawn Jamison drafted?
    A. Toronto
    B. Boston
    C. Orlando
    D. Minnesota

20. How many seasons did the Warriors spend in San Francisco before moving to Oakland?
    A. 6
    B. 7
    C. 9
    D. 11

21. Who was the last Warrior to be named MVP of the NBA All-Star Game?
    A. Rick Barry
    B. Chris Mullin
    C. Mitch Richmond
    D. Tim Hardaway

22. Wilt Chamberlain ranks second to which player in NBA career points?
    A. Michael Jordan
    B. Kareem Abdul-Jabbar
    C. Moses Malone
    D. Karl Malone

BONUS THREE-POINTERS

23. On February 15, 1989, the Warriors set an NBA record for most steals in one half with how many?
    A. 17
    B. 19
    C. 24
    D. 25

24. Which of the following Coach of the Year winners was once a first-round draft pick by the Warriors?
    A. Tom Heinsohn
    B. Doug Moe
    C. Gene Shue
    D. Lenny Wilkens

25. Who was the first player ever selected by the Warriors in the NBA Draft?
    A. Phil Farbman
    B. Francis Crossin
    C. Vern Gardner
    D. Ernie Beck

🏀 ANSWERS

1. B	10. B	19. A
2. C	11. C	20. C
3. D	12. B	21. A
4. B	13. B	22. B
5. A	14. A	23. A
6. D	15. A	24. C
7. B	16. B	25. B
8. D	17. C	
9. A	18. A	

HOUSTON ROCKETS

The Houston Rockets have soared in the 1990s, building upon their success in the '80s to become a championship team. Along the way, Houston's cast of characters has made the team a fan favorite around the league.

Free Throws

1. **In which city were the Rockets located before moving to Houston?**
    - A. San Francisco
    - B. San Diego
    - C. Kansas City
    - D. St. Louis

2. **Which team did the Rockets sweep in the 1995 NBA Finals?**
    - A. Orlando
    - B. New York
    - C. Indiana
    - D. Chicago

3. **Former Rocket Clyde Drexler went on to become the head coach at which college?**
   A. Rice
   B. Texas Tech
   C. University of Houston
   D. Texas—El Paso

TWO-POINTERS

4. **Rudy Tomjanovich is the winningest coach in Rockets history. Who is second?**
   A. Don Chaney
   B. Del Harris
   C. Bill Fitch
   D. John Egan

5. **Which Rocket holds the NBA record for highest free throw shooting percentage in a season at .958?**
   A. Rick Barry
   B. Sleepy Floyd
   C. Calvin Murphy
   D. Kenny Smith

6. **Who is the only Rockets player to win NBA MVP honors twice?**
   A. Hakeem Olajuwon
   B. Moses Malone
   C. Rudy Tomjanovich
   D. Charles Barkley

7. **Which of the following NBA coaches never played for the Rockets?**
   A. Pat Riley
   B. Rick Adelman
   C. Mike Dunleavy
   D. Chris Ford

8. To which team did the Rockets lose twice in the NBA Finals in the 1980s?
   A. Boston
   B. Detroit
   C. Philadelphia
   D. Washington

9. Which Houston player was a two-time winner of the NBA Defensive Player of the Year award?
   A. Scottie Pippen
   B. Moses Malone
   C. Rodney McCray
   D. Hakeem Olajuwon

10. Which Hall of Famer played the first four seasons of his career with the Rockets' franchise?
    A. Dave Bing
    B. Elvin Hayes
    C. Bill Walton
    D. Dave Cowens

11. Name the only player to win NBA Rookie of the Year honors as a Houston Rocket.
    A. Hakeem Olajuwon
    B. Clyde Drexler
    C. Ralph Sampson
    D. Moses Malone

12. Scottie Pippen was originally drafted by which team?
    A. Seattle
    B. Atlanta
    C. Chicago
    D. Houston

13. **Name the 1975 NBA Finals MVP known for his free throw shooting who finished his career in Houston.**
    A. Calvin Murphy
    B. Rick Barry
    C. Willis Reed
    D. John Havlicek

14. **Don Chaney won the NBA Coach of the Year award in 1990–91. Which Houston coach won the award in the 1970s?**
    A. Tom Nissalke
    B. Bill Fitch
    C. Tex Winter
    D. Alex Hannum

15. **Which Houston player was acquired in exchange for Sam Cassell, Chucky Brown, Robert Horry, and Mark Bryant?**
    A. Scottie Pippen
    B. Moses Malone
    C. Charles Barkley
    D. Clyde Drexler

16. **Who were the Twin Towers?**
    A. Moses Malone and Hakeem Olajuwon
    B. Ralph Sampson and Moses Malone
    C. Joe Barry Carroll and Chuck Nevitt
    D. Ralph Sampson and Hakeem Olajuwon

17. **Who was the first Rockets player who played his entire career with Houston to make it to the Hall of Fame?**
    A. Rudy Tomjanovich
    B. Calvin Murphy
    C. Moses Malone
    D. Mike Newlin

18. Name the player selected by the Rockets, after passing on Michael Jordan, with the first overall pick in the 1984 NBA Draft.
    A. Ralph Sampson
    B. Hakeem Olajuwon
    C. Kenny Smith
    D. Robert Horry

19. Whose number 45 jersey was retired by the Rockets?
    A. Rudy Tomjanovich
    B. Calvin Murphy
    C. Cliff Meely
    D. Otis Thorpe

20. Which of the following players was not selected first overall in the NBA Draft by the Rockets?
    A. Elvin Hayes
    B. Ralph Sampson
    C. Bobby Jones
    D. John Lucas

21. Houston tied the NBA record for most wins at the start of a season in 1993–94. How many games did they win before their first loss?
    A. 12
    B. 15
    C. 17
    D. 18

BONUS THREE-POINTERS

22. Hakeem Olajuwon holds the NBA record for most blocked shots in a career. Who ranks second?
    A. Mark Eaton
    B. Patrick Ewing
    C. Kareem Abdul-Jabbar
    D. Robert Parish

23. **Which year did the Rockets set an NBA record for most wins on the road in the playoffs with nine?**
   - A. 1981
   - B. 1986
   - C. 1994
   - D. 1995

24. **Rudy Tomjanovich was the starting power forward in the Rockets' first game in Houston on October 14, 1971. Where was that game played?**
   - A. Astrodome
   - B. The Summit
   - C. Astrohall
   - D. Houston Civic Center

🎾 ANSWERS

1. B	13. B
2. A	14. A
3. C	15. C
4. C	16. D
5. C	17. B
6. B	18. B
7. D	19. A
8. A	20. C
9. D	21. B
10. B	22. C
11. C	23. D
12. A	24. C

INDIANA PACERS

Located in the basketball hotbed of Indiana, the Pacers face high expectations from their fans. From the glory days of the ABA to the return of Larry Bird, Indiana has not disappointed Hoosier fanatics.

FREE THROWS

1. **Which Pacers player has a sister who is a head coach in the WNBA?**
    A. Antonio Davis
    B. Dale Davis
    C. Jalen Rose
    D. Reggie Miller

2. **The Pacers joined the NBA from the ABA in 1976. Which of the following teams was never in the ABA?**
    A. San Antonio Spurs
    B. New York Nets
    C. Denver Nuggets
    D. Dallas Mavericks

3. **Name the Pacers player who was the 1987 Rookie of the Year.**
   A. Chuck Person
   B. Mark Jackson
   C. Reggie Miller
   D. Rik Smits

Two-Pointers

4. **Which Pacer won back-to-back Sixth Man awards?**
   A. Vern Fleming
   B. Detlef Schrempf
   C. Herb Williams
   D. Wayman Tisdale

5. **In which country did center Rik Smits grow up?**
   A. Holland
   B. Denmark
   C. Sweden
   D. Norway

6. **Against which team did Reggie Miller score a stunning eight points in the final seconds of the game to capture a 107–105 playoff victory?**
   A. Chicago
   B. Orlando
   C. New York
   D. Atlanta

7. **Larry Bird won Coach of the Year honors for the Pacers in 1997–98. Which other Indiana coach has won that award?**
   A. Larry Brown
   B. Jack McKinney
   C. Jack Ramsay
   D. Dick Versace

8. **Pacers guard Mark Jackson attended St. John's University. Which of the following players did not play college basketball for the Red Storm?**
   A. Malik Sealy
   B. Jayson Williams
   C. Chris Mullin
   D. Kerry Kittles

9. **In which year were Pacers head coach Larry Bird and Chris Mullin Olympic teammates?**
   A. 1984
   B. 1988
   C. 1990
   D. 1992

10. **Which of the following players has not had his number retired by the Pacers?**
   A. George McGinnis
   B. Billy Knight
   C. Mel Daniels
   D. Roger Brown

11. **Beginning in 1999–2000, the Pacers are playing their home games at the new Conseco Field House. Which arena did Indiana call home for the previous 25 seasons?**
   A. Hoosier Dome
   B. Market Square Arena
   C. Bloomington Forum
   D. Indianapolis Civic Center

12. **Who is the Pacers' mascot?**
   A. The Gorilla
   B. The Coyote
   C. Boomer
   D. Rocky

13. **Who was the first Pacer ever voted to start in an All-Star Game?**
    A. Detlef Schrempf
    B. George McGinnis
    C. Mel Daniels
    D. Reggie Miller

14. **Mark Jackson has played for the Pacers on two separate occasions. With which of the following teams has he never played?**
    A. Los Angeles Clippers
    B. Denver Nuggets
    C. Charlotte Hornets
    D. New York Knicks

15. **Name the tallest player in Pacers history.**
    A. Derrick McKey
    B. Rik Smits
    C. Mel Daniels
    D. James Edwards

16. **The Pacers have been regulars in the NBA postseason. Name the first season that the team advanced beyond the first round.**
    A. 1980–81
    B. 1990–91
    C. 1993–94
    D. 1995–96

17. **Which of the following Pacers coaches guided the team in both the NBA and ABA?**
    A. Bob Leonard
    B. Larry Staverman
    C. George Irvine
    D. Dick Versace

18. **Name the first Pacers coach to coach the NBA Eastern Conference All-Star team.**
    A. Jack Ramsay
    B. Larry Bird
    C. Jack McKinney
    D. Bob Hill

19. **Derrick McKey and which other player were traded to Indiana for Detlef Schrempf in 1993?**
    A. Keith Smart
    B. Jerome Lane
    C. Gerald Paddio
    D. Lester Conner

20. **Austin Croshere was selected with which pick by Indiana in the 1997 NBA Draft?**
    A. 5
    B. 12
    C. 15
    D. 21

21. **How many ABA Championships did the Pacers win?**
    A. none
    B. 1
    C. 2
    D. 3

22. **What is Dale Davis's first name?**
    A. Elliott
    B. Randolph
    C. Everett
    D. Roland

BONUS THREE-POINTERS

23. **Before the Pacers, two other NBA teams called Indianapolis home. What were their nicknames?**
    - A. Jets and Olympians
    - B. Hoosiers and Indians
    - C. Hoosiers and Olympians
    - D. Jets and Indians

24. **Along with Julius Erving, which Pacer was named Co-MVP of the ABA in 1974–75?**
    - A. Mel Daniels
    - B. George McGinnis
    - C. Roger Brown
    - D. Bob Netolicky

25. **Pacers President Donnie Walsh played under which legendary coach in college?**
    - A. Adolf Rupp
    - B. John Thompson
    - C. John Wooden
    - D. Dean Smith

🎾 ANSWERS

1. D	10. B	19. C
2. D	11. B	20. B
3. A	12. C	21. D
4. B	13. D	22. A
5. A	14. C	23. A
6. C	15. B	24. B
7. B	16. C	25. D
8. D	17. A	
9. D	18. B	

LOS ANGELES CLIPPERS

The Los Angeles Clippers have worked hard to make a name for themselves in a city full of glamour and glitz. With an exciting young center around which to build, the team hopes to reward its loyal fans with great success in the next few seasons.

FREE THROWS

1. **Which other California city has the Clippers franchise called home?**
   - A. Oakland
   - B. San Diego
   - C. Sacramento
   - D. Fresno

2. **In 1998, center Michael Olowokandi became the second player in franchise history to be selected with the first overall pick in the draft. Name the first.**
   - A. Tom Chambers
   - B. Terry Cummings
   - C. Danny Manning
   - D. Hersey Hawkins

3. **Clippers Vice President Elgin Baylor had a Hall of Fame playing career with which NBA franchise?**
   A. Lakers
   B. Philadelphia
   C. New York
   B. Boston

TWO-POINTERS

4. **This Clipper finished his three-year college career as Cal's all-time leading scorer.**
   A. Lorenzen Wright
   B. Lamond Murray
   C. Maurice Taylor
   D. Rodney Rogers

5. **Under which name was the franchise known when it first entered the NBA in 1970?**
   A. Indianapolis Jets
   B. Buffalo Braves
   C. Cleveland Rebels
   D. Providence Steamrollers

6. **In which arena will the Clippers play their home games in 1999–2000?**
   A. Los Angeles Sports Arena
   B. Great Western Forum
   C. Pauley Pavilion
   D. Staples Center

7. **Which of the following players was not originally drafted by the Clippers?**
   A. Danny Ferry
   B. Byron Scott
   C. Billy Owens
   D. Adrian Dantley

8. **Which Clipper won Rookie of the Year honors in 1982–83?**
   A. Tom Chambers
   B. Terry Cummings
   C. Randy Smith
   D. Norm Nixon

9. **Name the franchise player who led the league in scoring for three straight seasons.**
   A. Ernie DiGregorio
   B. World B. Free
   C. Bob McAdoo
   D. Freeman Williams

10. **This Clipper won the Slam Dunk contest at the 1996 NBA All-Star Weekend.**
    A. Malik Sealy
    B. Terry Dehere
    C. Brent Barry
    D. Bo Outlaw

11. **Michael Cage led the league in this statistical category in 1987–88.**
    A. blocked shots
    B. minutes played
    C. three-pointers attempted
    D. rebounding

12. **Who is the Clippers' career leader in points?**
    A. Danny Manning
    B. Loy Vaught
    C. Randy Smith
    D. Bob McAdoo

13. **Which Clipper led the NBA in three-pointers made in the shot's first season?**
    A. Swen Nater
    B. Brian Taylor
    C. Freeman Williams
    D. Sidney Wicks

14. **On March 13, 1998, the Clippers set franchise marks in scoring, field goal percentage, and field goals made in a 152–120 victory over which team?**
    A. Toronto
    B. Orlando
    C. San Antonio
    D. Boston

15. **This Clipper had his college jersey number retired by Wake Forest in February 1997.**
    A. Brian Skinner
    B. Rodney Rogers
    C. Keith Closs
    D. Charles Smith

16. **Which player was named MVP of the 1978 NBA All-Star Game?**
    A. Randy Smith
    B. Bob McAdoo
    C. World B. Free
    D. Billy Knight

17. **Which former Clipper coach guided the team on two separate occasions in two different cities?**
    A. Bill Fitch
    B. Cotton Fitzsimmons
    C. Paul Silas
    D. Gene Shue

18. **In which division did the franchise play when it first entered the league?**
    A. Pacific
    B. Midwest
    C. Central
    D. Atlantic

19. **Which Clipper was named the 1989 Mississippi Player of the Year?**
    A. Pooh Richardson
    B. Eric Piatkowski
    C. James Robinson
    D. Darrick Martin

20. **In 1994, the Clippers traded Danny Manning to which team?**
    A. Phoenix
    B. Atlanta
    C. Seattle
    D. Miami

21. **Which player holds the franchise career record for blocked shots?**
    A. Bill Walton
    B. Benoit Benjamin
    C. Gar Heard
    D. Bob McAdoo

22. **Which former coach has the highest regular-season winning percentage with the franchise?**
    A. Larry Brown
    B. Jack Ramsay
    C. Mike Schuler
    D. Jim Lynam

BONUS THREE-POINTERS

23. Who was the first franchise player to participate in the NBA All-Star Game?

    A. Bob McAdoo

    B. Randy Smith

    C. Bob Kauffman

    D. Adrian Dantley

24. Which of the following players never played for the Clippers?

    A. Ozell Jones

    B. Wil Jones

    C. Charles Jones

    D. Willie Jones

25. Which of the NBA's yearly awards did Ernie DiGregorio win in 1973–74?

    A. Most Valuable Player

    B. Rookie of the Year

    C. Defensive Player of the Year

    D. Sixth Man award

🎾 ANSWERS

1. B	10. C	19. C
2. C	11. D	20. B
3. A	12. C	21. B
4. B	13. B	22. A
5. B	14. A	23. C
6. D	15. B	24. C
7. C	16. A	25. B
8. B	17. D	
9. C	18. D	

LOS ANGELES LAKERS

Amidst all the glitter and glitz of Hollywood, the Los Angeles Lakers have long been the glamour team of the NBA. The Lakers' stars come and go, but when the ball gets tipped, it's always showtime.

FREE THROWS

1. **In which city were the Lakers located before moving to Los Angeles?**
   - A. St. Paul
   - B. Minneapolis
   - C. Chicago
   - D. Cleveland

2. **Magic Johnson is the Lakers' all-time leader in assists and what other category?**
   - A. rebounds
   - B. minutes played
   - C. steals
   - D. scoring

3. **What college did Shaquille O'Neal attend?**
   A. Louisiana State
   B. Louisiana Tech
   C. Louisville
   D. Loyola Marymount

TWO-POINTERS

4. **Name the only player from the losing team ever to be named Finals MVP.**
   A. Wilt Chamberlain
   B. Jerry West
   C. Gail Goodrich
   D. Kareem Abdul-Jabbar

5. **The 1971–72 Lakers hold the NBA all-time record for the longest winning streak. How many consecutive games did they win?**
   A. 21
   B. 27
   C. 30
   D. 33

6. **Which of the following players was *not* selected by the Lakers with the first overall pick in the draft?**
   A. Elgin Baylor
   B. Jerry West
   C. Magic Johnson
   D. James Worthy

7. **Who is the Lakers' all-time leading rebounder?**
   A. Kareem Abdul-Jabbar
   B. Elgin Baylor
   C. Wilt Chamberlain
   D. Shaquille O'Neal

8. **Which Laker holds the NBA record for most blocked shots in a game?**
   A. Vlade Divac
   B. Kareem Abdul-Jabbar
   C. Shaquille O'Neal
   D. Elmore Smith

9. **Who was the last Laker to win the Defensive Player of the Year award?**
   A. Michael Cooper
   B. Kareem Abdul-Jabbar
   C. Wilt Chamberlain
   D. Jerry West

10. **Which of the following Lakers was named Rookie of the Year?**
    A. Magic Johnson
    B. Kobe Bryant
    C. Elgin Baylor
    D. James Worthy

11. **How many NBA titles did Pat Riley win as the head coach of the Lakers?**
    A. 2
    B. 3
    C. 4
    D. 5

12. **Which team drafted Kobe Bryant and traded his rights to the Lakers?**
    A. Charlotte
    B. Orlando
    C. Atlanta
    D. Miami

13. **Who was coaching the Lakers in the 1991 NBA Finals when they lost to Michael Jordan and the Chicago Bulls?**
    A. Pat Riley
    B. Del Harris
    C. Mike Dunleavy
    D. Paul Westhead

14. **Who was the Finals MVP when the Lakers beat the Pistons in 1988?**
    A. Magic Johnson
    B. James Worthy
    C. Byron Scott
    D. Kareem Abdul-Jabbar

15. **Led by Shaquille O'Neal, the Lakers had four players selected to the 1998 Western Conference All-Star team. Which of the following players did not join Shaq for the All-Star Game?**
    A. Kobe Bryant
    B. Eddie Jones
    C. Nick Van Exel
    D. Rick Fox

16. **Which of the following Lakers began his professional career with the Harlem Globetrotters?**
    A. Jamaal Wilkes
    B. Gail Goodrich
    C. Wilt Chamberlain
    D. Rudy LaRusso

17. **The Lakers held the record for most wins in a regular season with 69 until which team broke it?**
    A. Chicago Bulls
    B. Boston Celtics
    C. Philadelphia 76ers
    D. New York Knicks

18. Who is the Lakers' all-time leading scorer?
- A. Magic Johnson
- B. Jerry West
- C. Kareem Abdul-Jabbar
- D. Elgin Baylor

19. Which former Laker coach was selected by the Dallas Cowboys in the 1967 NFL Draft?
- A. Butch Van Breda Kolff
- B. Fred Schaus
- C. Pat Riley
- D. Mike Dunleavy

20. Who was the first Laker to win the NBA's Most Valuable Player award?
- A. George Mikan
- B. Elgin Baylor
- C. Gail Goodrich
- D. Kareem Abdul-Jabbar

21. Which former Laker broke the NBA record for most consecutive games played?
- A. Kurt Rambis
- B. A.C. Green
- C. Sam Perkins
- D. Mychal Thompson

22. Who holds the Laker record for most points scored in a single game (71)?
- A. Wilt Chamberlain
- B. Elgin Baylor
- C. Jerry West
- D. George Mikan

BONUS THREE-POINTERS

23. Happy Hairston played 395 games for the Lakers. What was his first name?

A. Henry

B. Harold

C. Herbert

D. Edward

24. Which Laker was the MVP of the 1953 NBA All-Star Game?

A. George Mikan

B. Slater Martin

C. Clyde Lovellette

D. Vern Mikkelsen

25. Which of the following players was not part of the trade that brought Wilt Chamberlain from Philadelphia to Los Angeles?

A. Jerry Chambers

B. Archie Clark

C. Darrall Imhoff

D. Tom Hawkins

● ANSWERS

I. B	10. C	19. C
2. C	11. C	20. D
3. A	12. A	21. B
4. B	13. C	22. B
5. D	14. B	23. B
6. B	15. D	24. A
7. B	16. C	25. D
8. D	17. A	
9. A	18. B	

MIAMI HEAT

For the last few seasons, one of the hottest teams in the NBA has been the Miami Heat. Led by one of the game's all-time greatest coaches, Pat Riley, the Heat have their aim fixed in one direction as they challenge for an NBA crown.

FREE THROWS

1. **Miami President and Head Coach Pat Riley earned his first NBA championship ring as a player with which team?**
   A. Houston Rockets
   B. Los Angeles Lakers
   C. Phoenix Suns
   D. New York Knicks

2. **Who led the Heat in scoring in 1997–98?**
   A. Glen Rice
   B. Tim Hardaway
   C. Alonzo Mourning
   D. Jamal Mashburn

3. **Which Miami player left the University of Texas–El Paso as the school's all-time leading scorer?**
   A. Tim Hardaway
   B. George Banks
   C. Alec Kessler
   D. Keith Askins

TWO-POINTERS

4. **Which Heat player won the Long Distance Shootout at the 1995 NBA All-Star Weekend?**
   - A. Steve Smith
   - B. Voshon Lenard
   - C. Dan Majerle
   - D. Glen Rice

5. **What is P.J. Brown's first name?**
   - A. Collier
   - B. Christopher
   - C. Connor
   - D. Conrad

6. **Tim Hardaway reached the 5,000-point, 2,500-assist mark in only 262 games. Who was the only player to reach that mark in fewer games?**
   - A. Magic Johnson
   - B. Oscar Robertson
   - C. Bob Cousy
   - D. John Stockton

7. **Which of the following players never scored 40 or more points in a game for the Heat?**
   - A. Rony Seikaly
   - B. Sherman Douglas
   - C. Glen Rice
   - D. Tim Hardaway

8. **Which Heat player was a two-time winner of the Slam Dunk contest at NBA All-Star Weekend?**
   - A. Billy Thompson
   - B. Harold Miner
   - C. Brent Barry
   - D. Pete Myers

9. **Only two rookies have played in all 82 games for the Heat in their first season. One is Grant Long. Name the other.**
   A. Sherman Douglas
   B. Kevin Edwards
   C. Bimbo Coles
   D. Rony Seikaly

10. **The 1992 NBA Playoffs marked the first time the Heat had made it to postseason competition. Which team did Miami play?**
    A. Chicago
    B. Indiana
    C. New York
    D. Orlando

11. **Who was the first coach of the Miami Heat?**
    A. Kevin Loughery
    B. Alvin Gentry
    C. Ron Rothstein
    D. Brendan Malone

12. **Which year did Miami host the NBA All-Star Weekend?**
    A. 1989
    B. 1990
    C. 1991
    D. 1992

13. **Name the Miami player who won the 1997 NBA Most Improved Player award.**
    A. P.J. Brown
    B. Dan Majerle
    C. Jamal Mashburn
    D. Isaac Austin

14. **Steve Smith and Grant Long were traded from Miami to Atlanta in 1994 in exchange for which player?**
    A. Matt Geiger
    B. Kevin Willis
    C. Billy Owens
    D. Khalid Reeves

15. **Which former Heat player was a starting guard for Yugoslavia in the 1996 Olympics?**
    A. Sasha Danilovic
    B. Vlade Divac
    C. Dino Radja
    D. Toni Kukoc

16. **Which of the following players never accumulated a triple-double for the Heat?**
    A. Rory Sparrow
    B. Steve Smith
    C. Billy Owens
    D. Glen Rice

17. **What is Dan Majerle's nickname?**
    A. Lightning
    B. Thunder
    C. Cyclone
    D. Tornado

18. **Which of the following players was not on Miami's roster for the team's inaugural season?**
    A. Craig Neal
    B. Ronnie Grandison
    B. Sylvester Gray
    C. Dwayne Washington

19. Name the former NBA Rookie of the Year who has served as an assistant coach with the Heat.
    A. Sidney Wicks
    B. Phil Ford
    C. Bob McAdoo
    D. Darrell Griffith

20. Which former Miami first-round draft choice played college basketball at Texas Christian?
    A. Kurt Thomas
    B. Willie Burton
    C. Dave Jamerson
    D. Harold Miner

21. Pat Riley holds the NBA record for most playoff coaching victories. Who ranks second?
    A. Chuck Daly
    B. Red Auerbach
    C. Phil Jackson
    D. Lenny Wilkens

22. Which Heat player collected 34 rebounds against Washington on March 3, 1993?
    A. Kevin Willis
    B. Issac Austin
    C. Alonzo Mourning
    D. Rony Seikaly

BONUS THREE-POINTERS

23. Name the Heat's first pick in the 1988 NBA Expansion Draft.
    A. Arvid Kramer
    B. Scott Hastings
    C. Hansi Gnad
    D. John Stroeder

24. **Which team did Miami beat on December 14, 1988 to claim its first NBA victory?**
    A. Dallas Mavericks
    B. Seattle SuperSonics
    C. Los Angeles Clippers
    D. New Jersey Nets

25. **Which NBA Hall of Famer was instrumental in bringing the Heat franchise to South Florida?**
    A. Bob Pettit
    B. Slater Martin
    C. Billy Cunningham
    D. Bill Walton

ANSWERS

1. B	14. B
2. C	15. A
3. A	16. D
4. D	17. B
5. A	18. B
6. B	19. C
7. C	20. A
8. B	21. C
9. C	22. D
10. A	23. A
11. C	24. C
12. B	25. C
13. D	

CHAPTER 15

MILWAUKEE BUCKS

The Milwaukee Bucks were quick to excel in the NBA, winning a title in only their third year in the league. Now Milwaukee fans have high hopes for the current Bucks to regain that championship form.

FREE THROWS

1. **Which Buck starred in the movie *He Got Game*?**
   - A. Glenn Robinson
   - B. Ray Allen
   - C. Vin Baker
   - D. Lee Mayberry

2. **Which team did George Karl coach just prior to coming to Milwaukee?**
   - A. Seattle
   - B. Golden State
   - C. Real Madrid
   - D. Albany Patroons

3. **What is Glenn Robinson's nickname?**
    A. Snoopy
    B. Big Bird
    C. Big Dog
    D. Batman

Two-Pointers

4. **Which team did the Bucks sweep to win their first NBA title in 1970–71?**
    A. Washington
    B. Baltimore
    C. Boston
    D. Los Angeles

5. **Kareem Abdul-Jabbar and Glenn Robinson were both first overall draft picks by Milwaukee. Which of the following players was also a first overall pick for the Bucks?**
    A. Julius Erving
    B. Quinn Buckner
    C. Sidney Moncrief
    D. Kent Benson

6. **Name the first coach of the Bucks.**
    A. Larry Costello
    B. Don Nelson
    C. Del Harris
    D. Gene Shue

7. **Which of the following players has *not* had his number retired by Milwaukee?**
    A. Brian Winters
    B. Jon McGlocklin
    C. Gary Brokaw
    D. Bob Lanier

8. **Which Buck won back-to-back NBA Defensive Player of the Year awards in 1983 and 1984?**
   A. Junior Bridgeman
   B. Marques Johnson
   C. Sidney Moncrief
   D. Alton Lister

9. **Which team traded Oscar Robertson to Milwaukee on April 21, 1970?**
   A. Cincinnati
   B. Buffalo
   C. Detroit
   D. Cleveland

10. **How many times did Kareem Abdul-Jabbar win the NBA MVP award as a member of the Bucks?**
    A. 2
    B. 3
    C. 4
    D. 5

11. **By which team was Ray Allen originally drafted?**
    A. Milwaukee
    B. Minnesota
    C. Phoenix
    D. Seattle

12. **George Karl was an All-America basketball player at which university?**
    A. Kentucky
    B. UCLA
    C. Syracuse
    D. North Carolina

13. **Name the Bucks' only two-time winner of the NBA Coach of the Year award.**
    A. Del Harris
    B. Mike Dunleavy
    C. Don Nelson
    D. Del Harris

14. **Which of the following Hall of Famers played for the Bucks?**
    A. Rick Barry
    B. Bill Walton
    C. Tiny Archibald
    D. Nate Thurmond

15. **Which of the following point guards was originally drafted by Milwaukee?**
    A. Terrell Brandon
    B. Stephon Marbury
    C. Kevin Johnson
    D. Mark Price

16. **Who was the first player selected by the Bucks in the NBA Draft who did not attend an American university or college?**
    A. Geert Hammink
    B. Dirk Nowitzki
    C. Mirsad Turkan
    D. Efthimis Retzias

17. **Which Buck won the NBA Sixth Man award in 1987 and 1990?**
    A. Ricky Pierce
    B. Terry Cummings
    C. Jack Sikma
    D. Randy Breuer

18. **Who scored the first four-point play in Bucks history?**
    A. Glenn Robinson
    B. Brian Winters
    C. Paul Pressey
    D. Frank Brickowski

19. **Name the player who finished his career with Milwaukee and went on to coach the Lakers, the Bucks, and the Trail Blazers.**
    A. Chris Ford
    B. Del Harris
    C. Mike Dunleavy
    D. Rick Adelman

20. **Which of the following records does Kareem Abdul-Jabbar *not* hold for the Bucks?**
    A. points
    B. rebounds
    C. field goal percentage
    D. free throw percentage

21. **On November 9, 1989, the Bucks beat which team 155–154 in a five-overtime game?**
    A. Seattle
    B. Philadelphia
    C. Cleveland
    D. Dallas

22. **Who is the Bucks' all-time leader in assists?**
    A. Oscar Robertson
    B. Paul Pressey
    C. Brian Winter
    D. Quinn Buckner

BONUS THREE-POINTERS

23. **Wisconsin had three pro basketball teams in the state prior to the Bucks. Which of the following teams never played in Wisconsin?**
    A. Madison Beavers
    B. Milwaukee Hawks
    C. Sheboygan Redskins
    D. Oshkosh All-Stars

24. **What was Junior Bridgeman's first name?**
    A. Randolph
    B. Ulysses
    C. Maxwell
    D. Harold

25. **On November 25, 1977, the Bucks came back from a 29-point deficit with 8:43 left in the game to beat which team in one of the NBA's greatest comebacks?**
    A. New York
    B. Boston
    C. Atlanta
    D. Portland

● ANSWERS

1. B	10. B	19. C
2. A	11. B	20. D
3. C	12. D	21. A
4. B	13. C	22. B
5. D	14. C	23. A
6. A	15. B	24. B
7. C	16. B	25. C
8. C	17. A	
9. A	18. B	

MINNESOTA TIMBERWOLVES

As the second NBA franchise to be located in the Twin Cities, the Minnesota Timberwolves had big shoes to fill. But as the Wolves begin their second decade in the league, this entertaining team has become a rising star and a fan favorite around the NBA.

FREE THROWS

1. **Minnesota Vice President of Basketball Operations Kevin McHale was an All-Star with which NBA team?**
   A. Los Angeles Lakers
   B. Philadelphia 76ers
   C. Boston Celtics
   D. Detroit Pistons

2. **Who was the first player in franchise history to be named an All-Star starter?**
   A. Tom Gugliotta
   B. Kevin Garnett
   C. Christian Laettner
   D. Stephon Marbury

3. **Which player representing the Timberwolves won the Slam Dunk contest at the 1994 NBA All-Star Weekend?**
   A. Spud Webb
   B. James Robinson
   C. Donald Royal
   D. Isaiah Rider

TWO-POINTERS

4. **Which team did Minnesota beat to win the franchise's first playoff game?**
   A. Boston
   B. Orlando
   C. Cleveland
   D. Seattle

5. **Which of the following CBA teams did Minnesota coach Flip Saunders not coach?**
   A. Albany Patroons
   B. Rapid City Thrillers
   C. La Crosse Catbirds
   D. Sioux Falls Skyforce

6. **Name the first Wolves player to record 1,000 points and 500 assists in his rookie season.**
   A. Christian Laettner
   B. Stephon Marbury
   C. Donyell Marshall
   D. Pooh Richardson

7. **Who was the first player from the Minnesota Timber-wolves to start in the NBA All-Star Game?**
   A. Tom Gugliotta
   B. Stephon Marbury
   C. Kevin Garnett
   D. Christian Laettner

8. **Christian Laettner was traded by Minnesota to Atlanta along with which other Wolves center?**
   A. Sean Rooks
   B. Stanley Roberts
   C. Randy Breuer
   D. Stojko Vrankovic

9. **Name the first coach of the Timberwolves.**
   A. Bill Blair
   B. Sidney Lowe
   C. Bill Musselman
   D. Jimmy Rodgers

10. **Which Timberwolves player was listed in *Newsweek* magazine as one of the 100 most influential people for the next decade?**
    A. Kevin Garnett
    B. Christian Laettner
    C. Tom Gugliotta
    D. Stephon Marbury

11. **Who was the first player selected by Minnesota in the 1989 NBA Expansion Draft?**
    A. Gary Leonard
    B. Doug West
    C. Rick Mahorn
    D. Felton Spencer

12. **Which Minnesota player was the first from Cuba ever to play in an NBA game?**
    A. DeJuan Wheat
    B. Andres Guibert
    C. Askia Jones
    D. Gundars Vetra

13. **Who scored 44 points against the Boston Celtics on February 2, 1990?**
    A. Tony Campbell
    B. Doug West
    C. Tyrone Corbin
    D. Stacey King

14. **Which of the following players never accumulated a triple-double for Minnesota?**
    A. Micheal Williams
    B. Tyrone Corbin
    C. Christian Laettner
    D. Kevin Garnett

15. **Minnesota selected Pooh Richardson with its first pick in its first NBA Draft in 1989. What is his first name?**
    A. Jerome
    B. Jeremy
    C. Jason
    D. Jasper

16. **When Luc Longley took the court for Minnesota on November 30, 1991, he was the first native of this country ever to play in the NBA.**
    A. France
    B. Belgium
    C. Canada
    D. Australia

17. As a senior, Flip Saunders teamed with Kevin McHale to lead which college to a then-school-record 24–3 season?
    A. Ohio State
    B. Minnesota
    C. Michigan
    D. Indiana

18. What other NBA franchise was once located in Minnesota before moving to its current location?
    A. Utah Jazz
    B. Los Angeles Clippers
    C. Atlanta Hawks
    D. Los Angeles Lakers

19. This player led the Timberwolves in total points scored for three straight seasons.
    A. Doug West
    B. Isaiah Rider
    C. Kevin Garnett
    D. Christian Laettner

20. Andrae Patterson was once named "Mr. Basketball" in which state?
    A. Indiana
    B. New York
    C. Texas
    D. New Jersey

21. Which player was originally signed by Minnesota in its first season and began his second stint with the team in 1995?
    A. Brad Lohaus
    B. Randy Breuer
    C. Sam Mitchell
    D. Brad Sellers

22. **Name Minnesota's career leader in points scored.**
    A. Doug West
    B. Isaiah Rider
    C. Tony Campbell
    D. Kevin Garnett

BONUS THREE-POINTERS

23. **Which nickname came in second when the Timberwolves were being named?**
    A. Owls
    B. Huskies
    C. Polars
    D. Blizzard

24. **Micheal Williams's NBA-record streak of 97 free throws ended against which team on November 9, 1993?**
    A. Dallas
    B. Golden State
    C. Miami
    D. San Antonio

25. **On April 17, 1990, the Timberwolves became the league's all-time single-season attendance champions, surpassing which team?**
    A. San Antonio
    B. Detroit
    C. Chicago
    D. Portland

🎾 ANSWERS

1. C	6. B	11. C	16. D	21. C
2. B	7. C	12. B	17. B	22. A
3. D	8. A	13. A	18. D	23. C
4. D	9. C	14. C	19. B	24. D
5. A	10. A	15. A	20. C	25. B

NEW JERSEY NETS

The Nets of the ABA were one of that league's most successful teams. With some of the most exciting and charismatic stars in today's NBA on their roster, the New Jersey Nets have a bright future ahead of them, as well.

FREE THROWS

1. **Name the Net who celebrated his first All-Star appearance at the 1998 All-Star Weekend in New York.**
   A. Kerry Kittles
   B. Kendall Gill
   C. Jayson Williams
   D. Rony Seikaly

2. **For which college team did Keith Van Horn star for four years?**
   A. Stanford
   B. Utah
   C. North Carolina
   D. Arizona

3. **Which Net was a three-time winner of the ABA MVP award?**
   A. Julius Erving
   B. Bill Melchionni
   C. John Williamson
   D. Rick Barry

Two-Pointers

4. **Which Nets coach went on to coach at St. John's University?**
   A. Bob MacKinnon
   B. Lou Carnesecca
   C. Bill Blair
   D. York Larese

5. **What is Stephon Marbury's hometown?**
   A. Brooklyn
   B. Queens
   C. Bronx
   D. Staten Island

6. **There were two Nets on the 1994 Eastern Conference All-Star team. One was Derrick Coleman. Name the other.**
   A. Mookie Blaylock
   B. Reggie Theus
   C. Buck Williams
   D. Kenny Anderson

7. **Which coach guided the Nets in both the ABA and NBA?**
   A. Max Zaslofsky
   B. Kevin Loughery
   C. Dave Wohl
   D. Stan Albeck

8. **This Net from Villanova was the first Wildcat in 25 years to earn First Team All-America honors from the Associated Press.**
   A. Tim Thomas
   B. Doug West
   C. Kerry Kittles
   D. Rory Sparrow

9. **Which Net set a New Jersey rookie scoring record with 1,909 points (24.2 ppg)?**
   A. Derrick Coleman
   B. Buck Williams
   C. Bernard King
   D. Kenny Anderson

10. **Before they were called the New York Nets, what was the ABA franchise called?**
    A. New York Monarchs
    B. New York Stormers
    C. New Jersey Bombers
    D. New Jersey Americans

11. **Which jersey number was retired in honor of Drazen Petrovic?**
    A. 3
    B. 4
    C. 23
    D. 25

12. **Who was the Nets' only first overall pick in the NBA Draft through 1998?**
    A. Sleepy Floyd
    B. Mookie Blaylock
    C. Buck Williams
    D. Derrick Coleman

13. **Which of the following players was *not* selected by the Nets in the ABA Draft?**
    A. Kareem Abdul-Jabbar
    B. Doug Collins
    C. David Thompson
    D. Bob Lanier

14. **Derrick Coleman was the NBA Rookie of the Year in 1990–91. Who was the first Net ever to win that honor?**
    A. Julius Erving
    B. Buck Williams
    C. Bernard King
    D. Chris Morris

15. **Before joining the Nets, Kendall Gill had two separate stints with this team.**
    A. Orlando
    B. Seattle
    C. Atlanta
    D. Charlotte

16. **Name the New Jersey player who left Miami as the Heat's all-time leader in rebounds and blocked shots.**
    A. Jack Haley
    B. Rony Seikaly
    C. Chris Dudley
    D. Shawn Bradley

17. **Who was the only Net to win ABA Rookie of the Year honors?**
    A. Brian Taylor
    B. Jim Chones
    C. Larry Kenon
    D. John Roche

18. **Name the Nets' all-time leading scorer.**
    A. Derrick Coleman
    B. Mike Gminski
    C. Buck Williams
    D. Chris Morris

19. **Which former Nets coach served as coach of the USA Men's Basketball team in the 1992 Olympics?**
    A. Chuck Daly
    B. Larry Brown
    C. Bill Fitch
    D. Willis Reed

20. **With which team did Jayson Williams begin his NBA career?**
    A. New York
    B. Philadelphia
    C. Cleveland
    D. Milwaukee

21. **In 1969–70, Nets Senior Vice President Willis Reed was MVP of the NBA's regular season, All-Star Game, and Finals. Who was the next player to accomplish this feat?**
    A. Magic Johnson
    B. Larry Bird
    C. Julius Erving
    D. Michael Jordan

22. **In which season did the Nets win their first ABA Championship?**
    A. 1969–70
    B. 1972–73
    C. 1973–74
    D. 1975–76

BONUS THREE-POINTERS

23. **Who holds the New Jersey record for most consecutive games played, with 319?**
    A. Armon Gilliam
    B. Darwin Cook
    C. Lester Conner
    D. Mike Gminski

24. **Which Net led the ABA in assists for three consecutive seasons?**
    A. Walt Simon
    B. Micheal Ray Richardson
    C. Bill Melchionni
    D. Kevin Porter

25. **On November 30, 1996, the Nets set an NBA record by scoring 25 points in one overtime period. Which team were they playing?**
    A. Los Angeles Clippers
    B. Denver Nuggets
    C. Sacramento Kings
    D. Portland Trail Blazers

● ANSWERS

1. C	10. D	19. A
2. B	11. A	20. B
3. A	12. D	21. D
4. B	13. C	22. C
5. A	14. B	23. B
6. D	15. D	24. C
7. B	16. B	25. A
8. C	17. A	
9. C	18. C	

NEW YORK KNICKS

Even among all the stars on Broadway, the New York Knicks have managed to shine. In a city filled with sports teams and sports fans, the Knicks have dominated both hearts and headlines for many years.

FREE THROWS

1. **Which Knick became a United States senator?**
   - A. Tom McMillen
   - B. Dave DeBusschere
   - C. Bill Bradley
   - D. Dick Barnett

2. **Where do the Knicks play their home games?**
   - A. Nassau Coliseum
   - B. Continental Airlines Arena
   - C. Madison Square Garden
   - D. 69th Regiment Armory

3. **Which flashy Knick playmaker was known as "Clyde"?**
   - A. Walt Frazier
   - B. Dick McGuire
   - C. Earl Monroe
   - D. Willie Naulls

TWO-POINTERS

4. **Name the Knick who won the Slam Dunk crown at the 1989 NBA All-Star Weekend.**
   A. Kenny Walker
   B. Gerald Wilkins
   C. Trent Tucker
   D. Johnny Newman

5. **The New York Knicks are one of three original franchises in the NBA. In fact, New York played in the first-ever NBA game. Name the Knicks' opponent that game.**
   A. Boston Celtics
   B. Philadelphia Warriors
   C. Chicago Stags
   D. Toronto Huskies

6. **In that game, who scored the league's first basket?**
   A. Harrry Miller
   B. Ossie Schectman
   C. Dolph Schayes
   D. Jake Weber

7. **Who was the coach of the Knicks for their two title runs in the '70s?**
   A. Red Holzman
   B. Fuzzy Levane
   C. Eddie Donovan
   D. Carl Braun

8. **Which Knick led the NBA in scoring in 1984–85 with an average of 32.9 points per game?**
   A. Bill Cartwright
   B. Bernard King
   C. Patrick Ewing
   D. Rory Sparrow

9. **Who has been the only Knick to win the NBA's Most Valuable Player award?**
   A. Walt Frazier
   B. Dick McGuire
   C. Patrick Ewing
   D. Willis Reed

10. **Which Knick won the NBA Sixth Man award in 1994–95?**
    A. Anthony Mason
    B. John Starks
    C. Charles Oakley
    D. Charlie Ward

11. **How many games were played in the 1994 NBA Finals matchup between the Knicks and the Rockets?**
    A. 4
    B. 5
    C. 6
    D. 7

12. **In which category is Patrick Ewing *not* the Knicks' all-time leader?**
    A. scoring
    B. steals
    C. free throw percentage
    D. rebounds

13. **How many seasons was Rick Pitino New York's head coach?**
    A. 1
    B. 2
    C. 3
    D. 4

14. **Which of the following Knicks did not win Rookie of the Year honors?**
    A. Willis Reed
    B. Walt Frazier
    C. Patrick Ewing
    D. Mark Jackson

15. **Who was the first coach of the Knicks?**
    A. Joe Lapchick
    B. Vince Boryla
    C. Ned Irish
    D. Neil Cohalan

16. **Who was the first Knick to score 50 or more points in a game?**
    A. Richie Guerin
    B. Harry Gallatin
    C. Cazzie Russell
    D. Jerry Lucas

17. **Against which team did the Knicks win their two NBA titles?**
    A. Seattle SuperSonics
    B. Golden State Warriors
    C. Los Angeles Lakers
    D. Portland Trail Blazers

18. **Which injured Knick hobbled out on the court in Game 7 of the 1970 NBA Finals, inspiring his team to victory?**
    A. Willis Reed
    B. Bill Bradley
    C. Dave DeBusschere
    D. Walt "Clyde" Frazier

19. **Which Knick led the league in both steals and assists in 1979–80?**
    - A. Sly Williams
    - B. Thomas Ray Williams
    - C. Walt Frazier
    - D. Micheal Ray Richardson

20. **New York won the first ever NBA Draft Lottery in 1985, enabling them to select which future Knick?**
    - A. Bernard King
    - B. Patrick Ewing
    - C. Mark Jackson
    - D. Kenny Walker

21. **Which Knick player went on to serve as the team's general manager from 1982–86?**
    - A. Ernie Grunfeld
    - B. Dave DeBusschere
    - C. Dick Barnett
    - D. Willis Reed

22. **Which number was retired to honor both Earl Monroe and Dick McGuire?**
    - A. 11
    - B. 15
    - C. 19
    - D. 21

BONUS THREE-POINTERS

23. **Which Knick was known by the nickname "Sweetwater"?**
    - A. Ken Sears
    - B. Nat Clifton
    - C. Willie Naulls
    - D. Ray Lumpp

24. **Which of the following Knicks did *not* go on to win NBA Coach of the Year honors?**
    A. Phil Jackson
    B. Richie Guerin
    C. Harry Gallatin
    D. Dave BeBusschere

25. **How many games did New York's legendary coach Red Holzman win with the Knicks?**
    A. 511
    B. 579
    C. 613
    D. 638

ANSWERS

1. C	14. B
2. C	15. D
3. A	16. A
4. A	17. C
5. D	18. A
6. B	19. D
7. A	20. B
8. B	21. B
9. D	22. B
10. A	23. B
11. D	24. D
12. C	25. C
13. B	

ORLANDO MAGIC

The Magic have become one of the most exciting attractions in Orlando since entering the league in 1989, making it to the NBA Finals in only their sixth season. A second-place finish that year only encouraged the team to set its sights even higher for the future.

FREE THROWS

1. **Which team did Orlando play against in the 1995 NBA Finals?**
   - A. Phoenix
   - B. Houston
   - C. Portland
   - D. Seattle

2. **Which player did the Magic select the first time they had the top overall pick in the NBA Draft?**
   - A. Chris Webber
   - B. Penny Hardaway
   - C. Shaquille O'Neal
   - D. Nick Anderson

3. **What is Penny Hardaway's first name?**
    A. Anfernee
    B. Anthony
    C. Avery
    B. Antonio

Two-Pointers

4. **Which player led the Magic in scoring in the team's first season?**
    A. Reggie Theus
    B. Otis Smith
    C. Jerry Reynolds
    D. Terry Catledge

5. **Name the player who won the NBA Most Improved Player award in 1990–91.**
    A. Jeff Turner
    B. Sam Vincent
    C. Dennis Scott
    D. Scott Skiles

6. **Who is the Magic's career leader in games played?**
    A. Nick Anderson
    B. Anthony Bowie
    C. Horace Grant
    D. Dennis Scott

7. **Which year did the Magic host the NBA All-Star Weekend?**
    A. 1991
    B. 1992
    C. 1993
    D. 1994

8. On April 18, 1996, the Magic's Dennis Scott set an NBA record by making how many three-pointers in one game?
   A. 11
   B. 12
   C. 13
   D. 14

9. What is the name of Horace Grant's twin brother, who is also an NBA veteran?
   A. Henry
   B. Harold
   C. Harvey
   D. Hank

10. Which Magic player had his college jersey number retired by Memphis State?
    A. Greg Kite
    B. Penny Hardaway
    C. Donald Royal
    D. Jeff Turner

11. Orlando's Matt Harpring was only the second player in Georgia Tech history to be named All-ACC First Team three straight seasons. Who was the first?
    A. Kenny Anderson
    B. John Salley
    C. Travis Best
    D. Mark Price

12. This player led the Magic in blocked shots, steals, and field goal percentage in 1997–98.
    A. David Benoit
    B. Charles Outlaw
    C. Gerald Wilkins
    D. Nick Anderson

13. **With which of the following CBA teams did Isaac Austin play in 1993—94?**
    A. Topeka Sizzlers
    B. Yakima Sun Kings
    C. Oklahoma City Cavalry
    D. Rockford Lightning

14. **Who was the head coach of the Magic in the team's first season?**
    A. Matt Guokas
    B. Bob Hill
    C. Brian Hill
    D. Chuck Daly

15. **How many NBA titles did Orlando's Horace Grant win with the Chicago Bulls?**
    A. 1
    B. 2
    C. 3
    D. 4

16. **Which Orlando player once was named the MVP of the Rookie Game at NBA All-Star Weekend?**
    A. Penny Hardaway
    B. Shaquille O'Neal
    C. Nick Anderson
    D. Dennis Scott

17. **At which college was Chuck Daly once the head coach?**
    A. Duke
    B. Pennsylvania
    C. Boston University
    D. Princeton

18. **Which Magic player set an NBA record with 30 assists in a single game?**
    A. Penny Hardaway
    B. Brian Shaw
    C. Sam Vincent
    D. Scott Skiles

19. **Who is Orlando's all-time leading scorer?**
    A. Shaquille O'Neal
    B. Dennis Scott
    C. Nick Anderson
    D. Penny Hardaway

20. **Which of the following players did not play for Orlando in its inaugural season?**
    A. Michael Ansley
    B. Morlon Wiley
    C. Mark Acres
    D. Tom Tolbert

21. **Which team did the Magic face when the team played two games in Japan in 1996?**
    A. New Jersey
    B. Seattle
    C. Houston
    D. New York

22. **Name the player whose draft rights were traded for Penny Hardaway and three future first-round picks.**
    A. Juwan Howard
    B. Chris Webber
    C. Shawn Bradley
    D. Shaquille O'Neal

Bonus Three-Pointers

23. Which of the following players never represented Orlando in the Slam Dunk contest at All-Star Weekend?
- A. Otis Smith
- B. Nick Anderson
- C. Darrell Armstrong
- D. Gerald Wilkins

24. Which player did Orlando choose with its first pick in the 1989 NBA Expansion Draft?
- A. Terry Catledge
- B. Reggie Theus
- C. Sidney Green
- D. Frank Johnson

25. Which team did the Magic beat for their first-ever victory?
- A. Philadelphia
- B. New York
- C. Miami
- D. Charlotte

⚾ ANSWERS

1. B		14. A	
2. C		15. C	
3. A		16. A	
4. D		17. B	
5. D		18. D	
6. A		19. C	
7. B		20. D	
8. A		21. A	
9. C		22. B	
10. B		23. D	
11. D		24. C	
12. B		25. B	
13. C			

PHILADELPHIA 76ERS

The Philadelphia 76ers have thrilled fans in the City of Brotherly Love with talented players and competitive basketball for decades. The club, founded in 1949, has been involved in some of the NBA's best rivalries and most exciting games.

FREE THROWS

1. **Who was the first Sixer ever to be named NBA Rookie of the Year?**
    A. Allen Iverson
    B. Charles Barkley
    C. Doug Collins
    D. Derrick Coleman

2. **In 1992, the Sixers acquired Jeff Hornacek, Tim Perry, and Andrew Lang from the Phoenix Suns for this one player. Who is he?**
    A. Hersey Hawkins
    B. Charles Barkley
    C. Jerry Stackhouse
    D. Maurice Cheeks

3. **Which player was known as "Doctor J"?**
   A. Luke Jackson
   B. Bobby Jones
   C. Wali Jones
   D. Julius Erving

Two-Pointers

4. **Which of the following franchises became the Philadelphia 76ers?**
   A. Anderson Packers
   B. Philadelphia Warriors
   C. Syracuse Nationals
   D. Rochester Royals

5. **Which former National became the first coach of the Philadelphia 76ers?**
   A. Henry Bibby
   B. Dolph Schayes
   C. Doug Collins
   D. Joe Bryant

6. **This successful NBA coach began his NBA career with the 76ers as an assistant coach in 1978. Who is he?**
   A. Chuck Daly
   B. Pat Riley
   C. Mike Dunleavy
   D. George Karl

7. **Who was the first Sixer to lead the NBA in scoring and rebounding in the same season?**
   A. Hal Greer
   B. Wilt Chamberlain
   C. Moses Malone
   D. Charles Barkley

8. **Which Sixer star went on to coach the Chicago Bulls and the Detroit Pistons?**
   A. Fred Carter
   B. Mike Dunleavy
   C. Doug Collins
   D. Phil Jackson

9. **What number did Charles Barkley wear as a Sixer?**
   A. 23
   B. 32
   C. 34
   D. 35

10. **Name the defensive star that won the NBA Sixth Man award in 1983.**
    A. Maurice Cheeks
    B. Rick Mahorn
    C. Moses Malone
    D. Bobby Jones

11. **Which team did Larry Brown coach before coming to Philadelphia?**
    A. Indiana Pacers
    B. Los Angeles Clippers
    C. San Antonio Spurs
    D. Denver Nuggets

12. **In 1983, Moses Malone predicted that the Sixers would sweep through the playoffs "Fo, fo, fo," but Philadelphia lost one game during that title run. Who beat them?**
    A. Los Angeles Lakers
    B. Milwaukee Bucks
    C. New York Knicks
    D. Boston Celtics

13. **What was the name of the longtime Sixer announcer whose microphone was retired in 1986?**
    A. Johnny Most
    B. Chick Hearn
    C. Dave Zinkoff
    D. Hot Rod Hundley

14. **When Maurice Cheeks retired in 1993, he was the league's all-time leader in which category?**
    A. steals
    B. assists
    C. free throws made
    D. free throws attempted

15. **Allen Iverson was the first overall pick in the 1996 NBA Draft. Name the player that Philadelphia selected the only other time it had the top pick.**
    A. Jerry Stackhouse
    B. Doug Collins
    C. Charles Barkley
    D. Shawn Bradley

16. **Name the former Sixer player and coach who was the ABA's MVP in 1972–73.**
    A. Paul Arizin
    B. Julius Erving
    C. Billy Cunningham
    D. Rick Barry

17. **Can you name the NBA team that the Philadelphia 76ers have to travel the longest distance to play? Hint: This team is 2,510 air miles away.**
    A. Vancouver
    B. Sacramento
    C. Portland
    D. Golden State

18. Which of the four basketball-playing Jones brothers played the first six years of his NBA career in Philadelphia?
    A. Caldwell
    B. Charles
    C. Major
    D. Wilbert

19. Philly native Wilt Chamberlain began his career with the Philadelphia Warriors. In 1962, the franchise moved to San Francisco and Wilt played two and a half seasons there before returning to his hometown during the 1964–65 season to play with the Sixers. He was the only non-guard ever to lead the league in assists; what season did he do this?
    A. 1965–66
    B. 1966–67
    C. 1967–68
    D. 1968–69

20. With which ABA team did Julius Erving begin his professional career?
    A. Virginia Squires
    B. Pittsburgh Pipers
    C. Memphis Pros
    D. Carolina Cougars

21. Who is the Sixers' all-time leading scorer?
    A. Dolph Schayes
    B. Hal Greer
    C. Julius Erving
    D. Charles Barkley

22. Which team did Philadelphia beat in the 1967 NBA Finals?
    A. Los Angeles Lakers
    B. St. Louis
    C. San Francisco
    D. Cincinnati

BONUS THREE-POINTERS

23. Which of the following Sixers did *not* win an NCAA Championship?
   A. Maurice Cheeks
   B. Henry Bibby
   C. Ed Pinkney
   D. Derek Smith

24. The Sixers played in the only game in NBA history in which some players played for both teams in the same game, owing to a protest, partial replay, and trade. Who was their opponent?
   A. Boston
   B. New Jersey
   C. New York
   D. Milwaukee

25. Dwight Wilber and Rory Sparrow are two of three players from Paterson Catholic High School in New Jersey to play for the Sixers. Name the more recent third.
   A. Allen Iverson
   B. Jerry Stackhouse
   C. Tim Thomas
   D. Jim Jackson

🏀 ANSWERS

1. A	10. D	19. C
2. B	11. A	20. A
3. D	12. B	21. B
4. C	13. C	22. C
5. B	14. A	23. A
6. A	15. B	24. B
7. B	16. C	25. C
8. C	17. B	
9. C	18. A	

PHOENIX SUNS

PHOENIX SUNS

Although they are still seeking their first NBA crown, the Phoenix Suns are always a dangerous opponent. Visitors to the Valley of the Suns know they have a battle on their hands when they step onto the court at America West Arena.

FREE THROWS

1. **What are the Suns' team colors?**
   - A. blue and yellow
   - B. gold and purple
   - C. orange, black, and purple
   - D. blue, green, and black

2. **Who is the Suns' mascot?**
   - A. The Coyote
   - B. The Gorilla
   - C. The Snake
   - D. The Scorpion

3. **Name the NBA coach who led the Suns in scoring for five straight seasons.**
   - A. Mike Dunleavy
   - B. Paul Westphal
   - C. Pat Riley
   - D. Kurt Rambis

Two-Pointers

4. As a Maverick, Jason Kidd shared NBA Rookie of the Year honors with which other player?
   A. Glenn Robinson
   B. Eddie Jones
   C. Juwan Howard
   D. Grant Hill

5. Phoenix coach Danny Ainge once played professional baseball for which organization?
   A. Boston Red Sox
   B. Toronto Blue Jays
   C. New York Yankees
   D. Baltimore Orioles

6. Which Sun star scored 15 consecutive points against the Golden State Warriors on December 22, 1992?
   A. Tom Chambers
   B. Dan Majerle
   C. Charles Barkley
   D. Jeff Hornacek

7. In the 1969 NBA Draft, the Suns lost a coin toss with Milwaukee for the number one pick. The Bucks selected Kareem Abdul-Jabbar. Which player did Phoenix choose at number two?
   A. Neal Walk
   B. Connie Hawkins
   C. Paul Silas
   D. Gail Goodrich

8. In which season did Charles Barkley win NBA MVP honors?
   A. 1989–90
   B. 1991–92
   C. 1992–93
   D. 1993–94

9. Name the Phoenix player who set an NBA playoff record by making nine three-pointers against Seattle on April 25, 1997.
   A. Cedric Ceballos
   B. Wesley Person
   C. Robert Horry
   D. Rex Chapman

10. Danny Manning won the 1998 NBA Sixth Man award as a member of the Suns. Which Phoenix player won that award in 1988–89?
   A. Dan Majerle
   B. Mark West
   C. Eddie Johnson
   D. Steve Kerr

11. Which Phoenix player set an NBA Finals single-game record for most minutes played with 62?
   A. Paul Westphal
   B. Alvan Adams
   C. Kevin Johnson
   D. Charles Barkley

12. Who is the only Suns coach to win the NBA Coach of the Year award?
   A. Cotton Fitzsimmons
   B. John MacLeod
   C. Paul Westphal
   D. Johnny Kerr

13. How many seasons did the Suns play at Veterans' Memorial Coliseum before moving to America West Arena?
   A. 15
   B. 18
   C. 21
   D. 24

14. **Which future Phoenix player led the ABA in scoring with 26.79 ppg in 1967–68?**
    A. Walter Davis
    B. Connie Hawkins
    C. Gail Goodrich
    D. Jim Fox

15. **When he took the court for Phoenix on March 2, 1997, Horacio Llamas became the first player from which country to play in an NBA game?**
    A. Mexico
    B. Venezuala
    C. Portugal
    D. Spain

16. **Alvan Adams was the 1976 NBA Rookie of the Year. Who is the only other player to win Rookie of the Year honors as a Sun?**
    A. Jason Kidd
    B. Larry Nance
    C. Walter Davis
    D. Gar Heard

17. **As a college senior, Tom Gugliotta was the only player in the country to lead his conference in both of these categories.**
    A. scoring and rebounds
    B. rebounds and three-pointers per game
    C. scoring and assists
    D. rebounds and free throw percentage

18. **Three Phoenix players were selected to play in the 1981 NBA All-Star Game. Which of the following players was not?**
    A. Walter Davis
    B. Paul Westphal
    C. Truck Robinson
    D. Dennis Johnson

19. **Jason Kidd broke which former Sun's career steals and assists record in two seasons at Cal–Berkeley?**
    A. Jay Humphries
    B. Kyle Macy
    C. Elliot Perry
    D. Kevin Johnson

20. **Danny Manning was the first overall pick in the 1988 NBA Draft by which team?**
    A. Los Angeles Clippers
    B. Atlanta Hawks
    C. Sacramento Kings
    D. Golden State Warriors

21. **Phoenix set an NBA record on April 9, 1990, with 61 of these.**
    A. assists
    B. rebounds
    C. free throws made
    D. personal fouls

22. **As a player with Orlando, Phoenix assistant coach Scott Skiles set an NBA record for most assists in a game with how many?**
    A. 25
    B. 28
    C. 30
    D. 33

BONUS THREE-POINTERS

23. **On November 10, 1990, the Suns set an NBA record by scoring 107 points in one half against which team?**
    A. Los Angeles Clippers
    B. Denver Nuggets
    C. Sacramento Kings
    D. Charlotte Hornets

24. Which of the following players was *not* selected by the Suns in the 1968 Expansion Draft?

A. Gail Goodrich
B. Dick Van Arsdale
C. John Wetzel
D. Gary Gregor

25. What is Cotton Fitzsimmons's first name?

A. Lowell
B. Lawrence
C. Leonard
D. Larry

ANSWERS

1. C	14. B
2. B	15. A
3. B	16. C
4. D	17. B
5. B	18. B
6. C	19. D
7. A	20. A
8. C	21. C
9. D	22. C
10. C	23. B
11. C	24. D
12. A	25. A
13. D	

CHAPTER 22

PORTLAND TRAIL BLAZERS

The Portland Trail Blazers have been blazing a trail through the Pacific Northwest. Title winners for the first time in 1977, the Blazers have assembled one of the league's most exciting teams to lead Portland into the next century.

FREE THROWS

1. At 7'3", who is the tallest player ever to take the court for the Trail Blazers?
    - A. Alaa Abdelnaby
    - B. Arvydas Sabonis
    - C. Sam Bowie
    - D. Petur Gudmundsson

2. Who was the MVP of the 1977 NBA Finals?
    - A. Bill Walton
    - B. Maurice Lucas
    - C. Lionel Hollins
    - D. Larry Steele

3. **Which Portland player was dubbed "The Wizard" in college?**
   A. Terry Porter
   B. Jerome Kersey
   C. Walt Williams
   D. Kiki Vandeweghe

TWO-POINTERS

4. **Who was the first Portland player to be selected to participate in an NBA All-Star Game?**
   A. Sidney Wicks
   B. Maurice Lucas
   C. Bill Walton
   D. Geoff Petrie

5. **Damon Stoudamire is the second Portland high school graduate to play for the Trail Blazers. Who was the first?**
   A. Steve Jones
   B. Kermit Washington
   C. Kenny Carr
   D. Darnell Valentine

6. **Name the youngest player to wear a Portland uniform.**
   A. Aaron McKie
   B. Byron Irvin
   C. Ron Lester
   D. Jermaine O'Neal

7. **Which year did Portland make Bill Walton the first overall pick in the NBA Draft?**
   A. 1973
   B. 1974
   C. 1975
   D. 1976

8. Which Portland coach was a member of the Philadelphia team which lost to Portland in the 1977 NBA Finals?
   A. Rick Adelman
   B. P.J. Carlesimo
   C. Mike Dunleavy
   D. Lenny Wilkens

9. Name the Trail Blazer who won the 1988 Most Improved Player award.
   A. Clyde Drexler
   B. Jerome Kersey
   C. Kevin Duckworth
   D. Kevin Gamble

10. Who was the last Portland coach to coach the Western Conference All-Star Team?
   A. Rick Adelman
   B. Jack Ramsay
   C. Mike Schuler
   D. Jack McCloskey

11. Which college has produced the most Trail Blazers?
   A. North Carolina
   B. Kentucky
   C. St. John's
   D. UCLA

12. Against Milwaukee on January 10, 1986, Clyde Drexler just missed recording a quadruple-double. In which category did he come up one short?
   A. points
   B. assists
   C. steals
   D. rebounds

13. **Geoff Petrie shared the NBA Rookie of the Year award in 1970–71. Which Portland player won that honor the following season?**
    A. Sidney Wicks
    B. Jim Barnett
    C. Lloyd Neal
    D. Bob Verga

14. **Which Blazer led the team in scoring from 1984–85 to 1986–87?**
    A. Clyde Drexler
    B. Mychal Thompson
    C. Kiki Vandeweghe
    D. Terry Porter

15. **Which player was traded with Clyde Drexler to Houston on Valentine's Day in 1995?**
    A. Otis Thorpe
    B. Tracy Murray
    C. Negele Knight
    D. Mark Bryant

16. **In which category did the Blazers set an NBA Finals record on June 14, 1992?**
    A. three-pointers made
    B. offensive rebounds
    C. free throws without a miss
    D. steals

17. **Which NBA award did Clifford Robinson win in 1992–93?**
    A. NBA Sixth Man award
    B. Most Improved Player
    C. Defensive Player of the Year
    D. J. Walter Kennedy Citizenship award

18. Who was Portland's first-round selection (17th overall) in the 1996 NBA Draft?
    A. Rasheed Wallace
    B. Jermaine O'Neal
    C. Brian Grant
    D. Isaiah Rider

19. Which of the following players has *not* had his number retired by the Blazers?
    A. Larry Steele
    B. Lloyd Neal
    C. Dave Twardzik
    D. Lionel Hollins

20. In addition to Bill Walton, the Blazers have had two other top picks in the NBA Draft. One was Mychal Thompson. Name the other.
    A. Clyde Drexler
    B. Walter Berry
    C. LaRue Martin
    D. Sam Bowie

21. From which country was Fernando Martin, who played for Portland in 1986–87?
    A. Mexico
    B. Brazil
    C. France
    D. Spain

22. Who was the first Portland coach to win NBA Coach of the Year honors?
    A. Rick Adelman
    B. Jack Ramsay
    C. Mike Schuler
    D. P.J. Carlesimo

BONUS THREE-POINTERS

23. When Rod Strickland wore number 1 for the Trail Blazers, he received permission from this man, in whose honor the number already had been retired.

    A. Jack Ramsay

    B. Larry Weinberg

    C. Harry Glickman

    D. Bill Schonely

24. Who was the first U.S. President to watch a Trail Blazers game in person?

    A. Gerald Ford

    B. Bill Clinton

    C. Jimmy Carter

    D. George Bush

25. Geoff Petrie is one of only eight players to score more than 2,000 points as a rookie. Which of the following players did *not* achieve that feat?

    A. Rick Barry

    B. Elvin Hayes

    C. Larry Bird

    D. Michael Jordan

● ANSWERS

1. B	10. A	19. D
2. A	11. D	20. C
3. C	12. D	21. D
4. D	13. A	22. C
5. A	14. C	23. B
6. D	15. B	24. A
7. B	16. C	25. C
8. C	17. A	
9. C	18. B	

SACRAMENTO KINGS

From Rochester to Cincinnati, from Kansas City to Sacramento, this franchise gradually made it all the way across the country. What began as the Royals is still royalty as the Kings. And in Sacramento, a young team with undeniable talent is ready to start a new winning tradition.

FREE THROWS

1. **Which team did Kings coach Rick Adelman lead to two NBA Finals appearances?**
    A. Detroit
    B. Portland
    C. Golden State
    D. Houston

2. **Which player from the Sacramento era was named MVP of the NBA All-Star Game?**
    A. Reggie Theus
    B. Lionel Simmons
    C. Mitch Richmond
    D. Pervis Ellison

3. The franchise changed nicknames from "Royals" to "Kings" because "Royals" was already being used in Kansas City. Which sport did the Royals play?

    A. baseball

    B. soccer

    C. football

    D. hockey

Two-Pointers

4. Tariq Abdul-Wahad was the first citizen of this country to play in the NBA.

    A. Portugal

    B. Belgium

    C. Switzerland

    D. France

5. Which Sacramento player appeared in the movies *Eddie*, *Driving Me Crazy*, and *Space Jam*?

    A. Walt Williams

    B. Vlade Divac

    C. Wayman Tisdale

    D. Reggie Theus

6. Name the King who was the first freshman ever to lead the Big Ten in rebounding.

    A. Chris Webber

    B. Randy Breuer

    C. Kevin Gamble

    D. Joe Kleine

7. **Celtic great Bob Cousy compiled a 141–209 regular-season record as coach of the Royals. Which other Boston star once served as head coach of the franchise?**
   A. John Havlicek
   B. Bill Russell
   C. Dave Cowens
   D. Nate Archibald

8. **The Rochester Royals beat which team in the 1951 NBA Finals?**
   A. Boston
   B. Fort Wayne
   C. New York
   D. Philadelphia

9. **Kings assistant coach Byron Scott won three NBA titles as a player with which team?**
   A. Chicago Bulls
   B. Los Angeles Lakers
   C. Boston Celtics
   D. Houston Rockets

10. **Which King was a high school classmate of Minnesota Vikings wide receiver Randy Moss?**
    A. Jason Williams
    B. Chris Webber
    C. Jon Barry
    D. Vernon Maxwell

11. **This Royals forward was named the 1956 NBA Rookie of the Year.**
    A. Jack Twyman
    B. Bobby Wanzer
    C. Don Meineke
    D. Maurice Stokes

12. Lawrence Funderburke graduated *magna cum laude* with a degree in business finance from which Big Ten college?
    A. Michigan
    B. Purdue
    C. Ohio State
    D. Iowa

13. Which of the following players was not selected by the Kings/Royals with the first overall pick in the draft?
    A. Pervis Ellison
    B. Rod Hundley
    C. Bob Boozer
    D. Jerry Lucas

14. Which Cincinnati player scored a franchise-record 59 points against the Lakers on January 15, 1960?
    A. Oscar Robertson
    B. Jack Twyman
    C. Wayne Embry
    D. Adrian Smith

15. At the 1990 NBA Draft, the Kings became the first team in history to select four players in the first round. Which of the four was picked first?
    A. Anthony Bonner
    B. Travis Mays
    C. Lionel Simmons
    D. Duane Causwell

16. Which jersey number was retired in honor of Hall-of-Famer Oscar Robertson?
    A. 14
    B. 17
    C. 21
    D. 26

17. **At the 1994 NBA All-Star Game, Mitch Richmond became the first King to start the game since which player?**
    A. Jimmy Walker
    B. Nate Archibald
    C. Sam Lacey
    D. Nate Williams

18. **Predrag Stojakovic was named MVP of which country's professional league in 1997–98?**
    A. Italy
    B. Spain
    C. France
    D. Greece

19. **This player once pulled down 40 rebounds in a game against Philadelphia.**
    A. Sam Lacey
    B. LaSalle Thompson
    C. Olden Polynice
    D. Jerry Lucas

20. **Which of the following players was not on the Kings' roster in the team's first season in Sacramento?**
    A. Billy Knight
    B. Otis Thorpe
    C. Eddie Johnson
    D. LaSalle Thompson

21. **Name the King who was voted Most Outstanding Player of the 1994 NCAA Tournament.**
    A. Bobby Hurley
    B. Corliss Williamson
    C. Tyus Edney
    D. Michael Smith

22. Who led the Kings in both rebounds and steals in 1997–98?
    A. Michael Stewart
    B. Olden Polynice
    C. Billy Owens
    D. Brian Grant

BONUS THREE-POINTERS

23. Which jersey number has been the most popular through-out the history of the Kings/Royals?
    A. 20
    B. 24
    C. 30
    D. 32

24. Who was coaching the franchise when the team won a record 55 games in 1963–64?
    A. Les Harrison
    B. Charles Wolf
    C. Jack McMahon
    D. Phil Johnson

25. From 1964 to 1966, the Cincinnati Royals produced three consecutive All-Star MVPs. Oscar Robertson and Jerry Lucas were the first two. Name the third.
    A. Happy Hairston
    B. Connie Dierking
    C. Adrian Smith
    D. Walt Wesley

● ANSWERS

1. B	6. A	11. D	16. A	21. B
2. C	7. B	12. C	17. B	22. C
3. A	8. C	13. D	18. D	23. A
4. D	9. B	14. B	19. D	24. C
5. B	10. A	15. C	20. A	25. C

CHAPTER 24

SAN ANTONIO SPURS

SAN ANTONIO SPURS

From the Iceman to the Admiral, San Antonio has had its share of outstanding players. And from the ABA to the NBA, the Spurs have made sure that the Alamo is not the only thing remembered in San Antonio.

FREE THROWS

1. **Which Spur served in the Navy for two years before joining San Antonio?**
   - A. George Johnson
   - B. David Robinson
   - C. Swen Nater
   - D. Rich Jones

2. **Which Spur won two rebounding titles in the '90s?**
   - A. Dennis Rodman
   - B. David Robinson
   - C. David Greenwood
   - D. Frank Brickowski

3. **Where did Tim Duncan grow up?**
   A. St. Thomas
   B. Jamaica
   C. Tortola
   D. St. Croix

TWO-POINTERS

4. **Which Spur won the NBA scoring title four times?**
   A. David Robinson
   B. George Gervin
   C. Artis Gilmore
   D. James Silas

5. **David Robinson won the 1992 NBA Defensive Player of the Year award. Which Spur won that award in 1985–86?**
   A. David Greenwood
   B. Johnny Dawkins
   C. Alvin Robertson
   D. Willie Anderson

6. **Which season did the Spurs move from HemisFair Arena to the Alamodome?**
   A. 1992–93
   B. 1993–94
   C. 1994–95
   D. 1995–96

7. **Name the only Spur to win the NBA MVP award.**
   A. Mike Mitchell
   B. David Robinson
   C. George Gervin
   D. Artis Gilmore

8. **At which sport did Tim Duncan excel before concentrating on basketball?**
   A. pole vault
   B. soccer
   C. baseball
   D. swimming

9. **Which of the following coaches never guided the Spurs?**
   A. Larry Brown
   B. Cotton Fitzsimmons
   C. Doug Moe
   D. Brian Hill

10. **Which team did Sean Elliott play for in between his two stints with the Spurs?**
   A. Detroit
   B. Houston
   C. Dallas
   C. Indiana

11. **Name the Spurs player who led the league in assists in 1981–82?**
   A. John Lucas
   B. Johnny Moore
   C. James Silas
   D. Wes Matthews

12. **From which ABA team did the Spurs acquire George Gervin?**
   A. Memphis Pros
   B. Washington Capitols
   C. Virginia Squires
   D. San Diego Conquistadors

13. **Which Spur was a two-time winner of the NBA steals title?**
    A. Johhny Moore
    B. Avery Johnson
    C. Mike Gale
    D. Alvin Robertson

14. **Which ABA and NBA All-Star holds the NBA career record for highest field goal percentage?**
    A. Jeff Ruland
    B. Artis Gilmore
    C. Bobby Jones
    D. Steve Johnson

15. **What number did George Gervin wear as a Spur?**
    A. 17
    B. 25
    C. 44
    D. 46

16. **Who was it that George Gervin battled for the NBA scoring title on the last day of the 1977–78 season?**
    A. Bob McAdoo
    B. Kareem Abdul-Jabbar
    C. David Thompson
    D. Calvin Murphy

17. **Which NBA coach led the league in three-point field goal percentage as a player with the Spurs in 1982–83?**
    A. Chris Ford
    B. Mike Dunleavy
    C. Jerry Sloan
    D. Rick Adelman

18. For which of the following teams has Avery Johnson *not* played?
    A. Seattle
    B. Denver
    C. Golden State
    D. Charlotte

19. Name the player who was San Antonio's top draft pick in the 1998 NBA Draft.
    A. Felipe Lopez
    B. Bryce Drew
    C. Corey Benjamin
    D. Derrick Dial

20. What well-known college coach briefly led the Spurs in the 1992–93 season?
    A. Larry Brown
    B. Rick Pitino
    C. George Raveling
    D. Jerry Tarkanian

21. Whose nickname was "Iceman"?
    A. Artis Gilmore
    B. George Gervin
    C. Johnny Moore
    D. Larry Kenon

22. Which Spur wore jersey number 13, the first number ever retired by San Antonio?
    A. James Silas
    B. Swen Nater
    C. Billy Paultz
    D. Mike Gale

BONUS THREE-POINTERS

23. Which player did the Spurs select in the 1976 Dispersal Draft prior to joining the NBA?
A. Louie Dampier
B. Artis Gilmore
C. Marvin Barnes
D. Moses Malone

24. In which city were the ABA Spurs located before moving to San Antonio?
A. Houston
B. Dallas
C. Pittsburgh
D. New Orleans

25. What was that team's nickname?
A. Pipers
B. Condors
C. Stars
D. Chaparrals

● ANSWERS

1.	B	14.	B
2.	A	15.	C
3.	D	16.	C
4.	B	17.	B
5.	C	18.	D
6.	B	19.	A
7.	B	20.	D
8.	D	21.	B
9.	D	22.	A
10.	A	23.	A
11.	B	24.	B
12.	C	25.	D
13.	D		

SEATTLE SUPERSONICS

Super in Seattle is how the Seattle SuperSonics should be known. For years now, the team has been one of the best in the Western Conference, and the Sonics always seems to be a legitimate contender for the NBA crown.

FREE THROWS

1. **Where did the Sonics play while KeyArena was being built?**
    A. Kingdome
    B. Tacoma Dome
    C. The Seattle Center
    D. University of Washington

2. **Which former Seattle player and coach is the NBA's all-time leader in coaching victories?**
    A. Red Auerbach
    B. Bill Fitch
    C. Lenny Wilkens
    D. Bernie Bickerstaff

3. **Which Sonic became known as "The Glove"?**
   A. Xavier McDaniel
   B. Nate McMillan
   C. Sedale Threatt
   D. Gary Payton

Two-Pointers

4. **With which team did Sonics coach Paul Westphal win an NBA title as a player?**
   A. Phoenix Suns
   B. Los Angeles Lakers
   C. Philadelphia 76ers
   D. Boston Celtics

5. **Vin Baker had his college jersey retired by which college in January, 1998?**
   A. Maryland
   B. Hartford
   C. Auburn
   D. Northeastern

6. **Name the Sonic who set an NBA record by playing 69 minutes in a single game.**
   A. Dale Ellis
   B. Ricky Pierce
   C. Derrick McKey
   D. Michael Cage

7. **Which of the following players has *not* had his number retired by the Sonics?**
   A. Fred Brown
   B. Lenny Wilkens
   C. Jack Sikma
   D. Dennis Johnson

8. **At the 1987 All-Star Game in Seattle, which Sonic won MVP honors?**
    A. Nate McMillan
    B. Tom Chambers
    C. Dae Ellis
    D. Xavier McDaniel

9. **Sonics assistant coach Nate McMillan retired as Seattle's all-time leader in which categories?**
    A. assists and steals
    B. games played and games started
    C. free throws made and attempted
    D. rebounds and blocked shots

10. **Which team did the Sonics beat to win their first NBA title in 1979?**
    A. Boston
    B. Philadelphia
    C. Washington
    D. Milwaukee

11. **Who was the Finals MVP that season?**
    A. Gus Williams
    B. Fred Brown
    C. Jack Sikma
    D. Dennis Johnson

12. **Throughout 1998, the Sonics had never had the first overall pick in the NBA Draft. Which player did they choose with their highest pick ever, at number 2?**
    A. Lucius Allen
    B. Scottie Pippen
    C. Gary Payton
    D. Vinnie Johnson

13. **Which Sonic hit an amazing eight three-pointers without a miss on January 15, 1997?**
    A. Sam Perkins
    B. Dale Ellis
    C. Dana Barros
    D. Hersey Hawkins

14. **K.C. Jones coached the Sonics in the early '90s. Which of the following Celtic stars also once served as Seattle's head coach?**
    A. John Havlicek
    B. Bill Russell
    C. Dave Cowens
    D. Tom Sanders

15. **"Downtown" Freddie Brown set the single-game scoring record for the Sonics with how many points against Golden State on March 23, 1974?**
    A. 58
    B. 61
    C. 65
    D. 69

16. **Detlef Schrempf is a native of Leverkusen, Germany, but attended high school and college in which U.S. state?**
    A. Indiana
    B. Washington
    C. Florida
    D. California

17. **Seattle was defeated by Chicago in the 1996 Finals in how many games?**
    A. 4
    B. 5
    C. 6
    D. 7

18. **Name the Sonic who led the league in assists and steals in 1975–76.**
    A. Dennis Johnson
    B. Slick Watts
    C. Mike Green
    D. Dick Snyder

19. **Which college did Jack Sikma attend?**
    A. Illinois Wesleyan
    B. Fresno State
    C. Creighton
    D. Washington State

20. **Which player did the Sonics send to Cleveland in exchange for Vin Baker in the three-team trade with the Cavs and the Bucks?**
    A. Derrick McKey
    B. Kendall Gill
    C. Jim McIlvaine
    D. Shawn Kemp

21. **Who was the first Seattle SuperSonic to ever start in three consecutive NBA All-Star Games?**
    A. Shawn Kemp
    B. Detlef Schrempf
    C. Clyde Drexler
    D. Nate McMillan

22. **Which Sonic once made 75 consecutive free throws?**
    A. Ricky Pierce
    B. Gus Williams
    C. Hersey Hawkins
    D. John Johnson

BONUS THREE-POINTERS

23. Name the first coach of the Sonics.
    A. Bob Hopkins
    B. Al Bianchi
    C. Tom Nissalke
    D. Bucky Buckwalter

24. What was Slick Watts's first name?
    A. Don
    B. Dave
    C. Dan
    D. Dean

25. In 1993–94, Seattle averaged 12.8 steals per game, the second-highest steals average in NBA history. Who ranks first?
    A. Denver
    B. Phoenix
    C. Golden State
    D. Sacramento

● ANSWERS

1. B	14. B
2. C	15. A
3. D	16. B
4. D	17. C
5. B	18. B
6. A	19. A
7. D	20. D
8. B	21. A
9. A	22. A
10. C	23. B
11. D	24. A
12. C	25. B
13. A	

CHAPTER

26

TORONTO RAPTORS

The NBA began in Toronto in 1946 and returned with the Raptors in 1995. In a country known more for other sports, the Toronto Raptors have won hearts and fans, encouraging a whole new generation of basketball players.

FREE THROWS

1. **Where did the Raptors play their home games during their first few seasons in the NBA?**
   A. Maple Leaf Gardens
   B. SkyDome
   C. Toronto Convention Center
   D. Air Canada Centre

2. **Which Raptor won NBA Rookie of the Year honors?**
   A. Damon Stoudamire
   B. Marcus Camby
   C. Doug Christie
   D. John Wallace

3. **Which NBA All-Star was a front office executive with Toronto?**
   A. Magic Johnson
   B. Dave Bing
   C. Isiah Thomas
   D. Julius Erving

TWO-POINTERS

4. **Which team did the Raptors play to tip off the NBA's fiftieth anniversary season?**
   A. New York
   B. Vancouver
   C. Detroit
   D. Boston

5. **Who was the Raptors' first pick in the 1995 NBA Expansion Draft?**
   A. Jerome Kersey
   B. Willie Anderson
   C. John Salley
   D. B.J. Armstrong

6. **Name the first coach of the Raptors.**
   A. Isiah Thomas
   B. Darrell Walker
   C. Brendan Malone
   D. Brendan Suhr

7. **With which team did Charles Oakley first play in the NBA?**
   A. Chicago
   B. Cleveland
   C. New York
   D. Toronto

8. **Which Raptor participated in the Schick Rookie Game during the 1998 NBA All-Star Weekend?**
    A. Doug Christie
    B. Tracy McGrady
    C. Marcus Camby
    D. Damon Stoudamire

9. **How many victories did Toronto compile in its first NBA season?**
    A. 15
    B. 18
    C. 21
    D. 25

10. **Which of the following players was *not* in the starting lineup for the Raptors in their first-ever game?**
    A. Zan Tabak
    B. Hubert Davis
    C. Carlos Rogers
    D. Ed Pinckney

11. **When the NBA Draft was held in Toronto, it was the first time it had been held outside of the U.S. Which year was that?**
    A. 1993
    B. 1994
    C. 1995
    D. 1996

12. **As a senior in high school, John Wallace was named "Mr. Basketball" of which state?**
    A. New York
    B. Indiana
    C. Illinois
    D. Kentucky

13. **Which title did Dee Brown win at the 1991 NBA All-Star Weekend in Charlotte?**
    A. Rookie Game MVP
    B. Slam Dunk Champion
    C. Long Distance Shootout Champion
    D. All-Star Game MVP

14. **Toronto acquired Vince Carter from Golden State in exchange for the draft rights to which player?**
    A. Tyson Wheeler
    B. Larry Hughes
    C. Keon Clark
    D. Antawn Jamison

15. **Which Raptor tied an NBA record with eight steals in a half?**
    A. Damon Stoudamire
    B. Doug Christie
    C. Dee Brown
    D. Hubert Davis

16. **Which player set a Toronto record with 51 consecutive free throws made?**
    A. Kevin Willis
    B. Charles Oakley
    C. Chauncey Billups
    D. Walt Williams

17. **What was the nickname of the first professional basketball team in Toronto?**
    A. Bulldogs
    B. Bears
    C. Cougars
    D. Huskies

18. Toronto coach Butch Carter's brother Cris is a wide receiver with which NFL team?
    A. Minnesota
    B. Green Bay
    C. Dallas
    D. Oakland

19. Name the Raptor who led the NBA in blocked shots in 1997–98.
    A. Oliver Miller
    B. Marcus Camby
    C. John Wallace
    D. Carlos Rogers

20. By which team was Doug Christie originally drafted?
    A. New York Knicks
    B. Seattle SuperSonics
    C. Los Angeles Lakers
    D. Los Angeles Clippers

21. Which Toronto player developed his own clothing line?
    A. Alvin Robertson
    B. Tony Massenburg
    C. Gary Trent
    D. Kevin Willis

22. Who is the oldest player to play for the Raptors?
    A. Earl Cureton
    B. Alvin Robertson
    C. John Long
    D. Herb Williams

BONUS THREE-POINTERS

23. Name the player who collected 21 rebounds for Toronto on December 10, 1996, against Boston.
    A. Oliver Miller
    B. Kevin Willis
    C. Popeye Jones
    D. Marcus Camby

24. In 1996–97, the Raptors were one of only four teams to beat each of the top three teams in the league that season—Chicago, Utah, and Miami. Which of the following teams did not accomplish that feat?
    A. New York
    B. Atlanta
    C. Lakers
    D. Orlando

25. Which Raptor participated in the Long Distance Shootout at the 1997 NBA All-Star Weekend?
    A. Walt Williams
    B. Cliff Rozier
    C. Shawn Respert
    D. Damon Stoudamire

● ANSWERS

1. B	10. B	19. B
2. A	11. C	20. B
3. C	12. A	21. D
4. A	13. B	22. C
5. D	14. D	23. C
6. C	15. B	24. D
7. A	16. C	25. A
8. B	17. D	
9. C	18. A	

CHAPTER 27

UTAH JAZZ

In scenic Salt Lake City, Utah has been one of the league's most consistent teams in recent years. From Maravich to Stockton and Malone, the Jazz have made beautiful music on the court.

FREE THROWS

1. **In which city known for music was the Jazz located before moving to Salt Lake?**
   A. Memphis
   B. Nashville
   C. Austin
   D. New Orleans

2. **What is Karl Malone's nickname?**
   A. The Mailman
   B. The Postman
   C. Special Delivery
   D. Express Mail

3. **Where did the Jazz play before moving to the Delta Center in 1991–92?**
   A. The Palace of Auburn Hills
   B. The Salt Palace
   C. Utah Civic Center
   D. Salt Lake Arena

TWO-POINTERS

4. **In 1974, Pete Maravich joined the Jazz. He came via a trade with which team?**
   A. Atlanta
   B. Detroit
   C. New Jersey
   D. Philadelphia

5. **Which Jazz player won back-to-back Defensive Player of the Year awards?**
   A. Leonard Robinson
   B. Rich Kelly
   C. Mark Eaton
   D. Danny Schayes

6. **Whose career assists mark did John Stockton break to set a new NBA record?**
   A. Oscar Robertson
   B. Magic Johnson
   C. Isiah Thomas
   D. Lenny Wilkens

7. **Name the Jazz player who won the Comeback Player of the Year award in 1983–84. (The Comeback Player of the Year award is now called the Most Improved Player award.)**
   A. Jay Humphries
   B. Thurl Bailey
   C. Tom Chambers
   D. Adrian Dantley

8. **Which team did Utah face in its consecutive trips to the NBA Finals in 1997 and 1998?**
   A. Detroit
   B. Chicago
   C. Boston
   D. Philadelphia

9. **Only one Jazz player has won the Rookie of the Year award. Who's that?**
   A. Darrell Griffith
   B. Karl Malone
   C. Pete Maravich
   D. Mark Eaton

10. **Which of the following players was originally drafted by the Jazz?**
    A. Joe Dumars
    B. Scottie Pippen
    C. Dominique Wilkins
    D. Mark Price

11. **At which All-Star Weekend did John Stockton and Karl Malone win co-MVP awards?**
    A. 1989
    B. 1991
    C. 1992
    D. 1993

12. **Jazz guard Jeff Hornacek was drafted by the Phoenix Suns and played six seasons there. In 1992, he was traded along with Andrew Lang and Tim Perry to Philadelphia for one player. Who was that?**
    A. Charles Barkley
    B. Derrick Coleman
    C. Moses Malone
    D. Andrew Toney

13. **Which Jazz player won the NBA scoring title in 1980–81 with an average of 30.7 points per game?**
    A. Pete Maravich
    B. Adrian Dantley
    C. Karl Malone
    D. John Stockton

14. **John Stockton, his father, and his grandfather all attended this college.**
    A. Georgetown
    B. George Washington
    C. Gonzaga
    D. Georgia Tech

15. **Coach Jerry Sloan was a two-time All-Star with which NBA team?**
    A. Chicago
    B. New York
    C. Boston
    D. Philadelphia

16. **Pete Maravich went to the same college as which of these other NBA players?**
    A. Reggie Miller
    B. Shaquille O'Neal
    C. Grant Hill
    D. Antoine Walker

17. **Which of the following coaches was the first in Jazz franchise history?**
    A. Tom Nissalke
    B. Scotty Robertson
    C. Bill van Breda Kolff
    D. Frank Layden

18. **Mark Eaton holds the Jazz career record in this category.**
    A. rebounds
    B. minutes played
    C. games played
    D. blocked shots

19. **For how many consecutive seasons did John Stockton lead the NBA in assists?**
    A. 7
    B. 8
    C. 9
    D. 11

20. **He is the only player who has won the NBA MVP award as a member of the Jazz.**
    A. John Stockton
    B. Karl Malone
    C. Adrian Dantley
    D. Pete Maravich

21. **Name the winningest coach in Jazz history.**
    A. Frank Layden
    B. Scott Layden
    C. Elgin Baylor
    D. Jerry Sloan

22. **Pete Maravich set the all-time Jazz record for most points scored in a single game with how many?**
    A. 68
    B. 65
    C. 61
    D. 58

BONUS THREE-POINTERS

23. **Leonard Robinson was one of the Jazz's top rebounders in the team's early years. What was his nickname?**
    A. Big Dog
    B. Truck
    C. Crash
    D. Big Bells

24. **What was the name of the ABA team that played in Utah before the Jazz arrived?**
    A. Pros
    B. Condors
    C. Stars
    D. Pipers

25. **Name the former Jazz player who set a professional basketball record by playing in 1,041 consecutive games.**
    A. Ron Boone
    B. Gail Goodrich
    C. Danny Schayes
    D. Thurl Bailey

◐ ANSWERS

1. D	14. C
2. A	15. A
3. B	16. B
4. A	17. B
5. C	18. D
6. B	19. C
7. D	20. B
8. B	21. D
9. A	22. D
10. C	23. B
11. D	24. C
12. A	25. A
13. B	

VANCOUVER GRIZZLIES

The scenic city of Vancouver welcomed the Grizzlies eagerly in the league's most recent expansion. Throughout British Columbia, Grizzlies fans cheer and support their young players as they develop into NBA veterans.

FREE THROWS

1. **What other NBA franchise entered the league the same season as the Grizzlies?**
   - A. Minnesota Timberwolves
   - B. Orlando Magic
   - C. Toronto Raptors
   - D. Charlotte Hornets

2. **Vancouver President and General Manager Stu Jackson is a former head coach of which NBA team?**
   - A. New Jersey
   - B. New York
   - C. Portland
   - D. Seattle

3. **Which Vancouver player is known as "Big Country"?**
   A. Bryant Reeves
   B. Cherokee Parks
   C. Michael Smith
   D. Pete Chilcutt

Two-Pointers

4. **Which team did the Grizzlies defeat for their first-ever victory?**
   A. Toronto
   B. Miami
   C. Dallas
   D. Portland

5. **Name the first player selected by Vancouver in the 1995 NBA Expansion Draft.**
   A. Blue Edwards
   B. Greg Anthony
   C. Doug Edwards
   D. Kenny Gattison

6. **Who was the first head coach of the Grizzlies?**
   A. Brian Hill
   B. Bob Hill
   C. Brian Winters
   D. Lionel Hollins

7. **Which Grizzlies player was the only unanimous selection to the All-Rookie First Team in 1996–97?**
   A. Bryant Reeves
   B. Lee Mayberry
   C. Shareef Abdur-Rahim
   D. Lawrence Moten

8. **Which of the following players has *not* played for Vancouver?**
   A. Otis Thorpe
   B. Byron Scott
   C. Gerald Wilkins
   D. Charles Smith

9. **This Vancouver player led the Big East in rebounding in each of his three college seasons.**
   A. Michael Smith
   B. Doug West
   C. Eric Murdock
   D. Chris King

10. **Which year was the NBA Draft held at Vancouver's General Motors Place?**
    A. 1996
    B. 1997
    C. 1998
    D. 1999

11. **Which Grizzlies player wore jersey number 00?**
    A. Benoit Benjamin
    B. Eric Mobley
    C. Eric Leckner
    D. Rich Manning

12. **Name the Grizzlies player who was a member of the 1992 NCAA Champions.**
    A. George Lynch
    B. Cherokee Parks
    C. Pete Chilcutt
    D. Greg Anthony

13. Blue Edwards played in 96 straight games for Vancouver. What is his first name?
    A. Thaddeus
    B. Terrence
    C. Theodore
    D. Terrell

14. Which Grizzlies player entered the 1996 NBA Draft after playing at California?
    A. Shareef Abdur-Rahim
    B. Tony Massenburg
    C. Anthony Avent
    D. Felipe Lopez

15. Name the Grizzlies player who scored 40 points at New Jersey on February 4, 1997.
    A. Anthony Peeler
    B. Bryant Reeves
    C. Byron Scott
    D. Tony Massenburg

16. He was the first freshman ever to win Pac–10 Player of the Year honors.
    A. Rich Manning
    B. Eric Leckner
    C. Darrick Martin
    D. Shareef Abdur-Rahim

17. Bryant Reeves was the first Vancouver player selected to play in the Rookie Game at the NBA All-Star Weekend. Which of the following players was *not* picked to play in that game?
    A. Roy Rogers
    B. Antonio Daniels
    C. Chris Robinson
    D. Shareef Abdur-Rahim

18. The Grizzlies set an NBA record for most free throws attempted in one quarter on November 11, 1997, against the Clippers. How many did Vancouver shoot?
    A. 28
    B. 32
    C. 37
    D. 41

19. Which nickname was almost given to the Vancouver franchise?
    A. Falcons
    B. Rebels
    C. Mounties
    D. Stags

20. On January 7, 1996, two thousand Vancouver fans got their hair cut in the same style as which Grizzlies player?
    A. Kenny Gattison
    B. Bryant Reeves
    C. Eric Mobley
    D. Benoit Benjamin

21. Name the first player Vancouver selected in the 1998 NBA Draft.
    A. Antawn Jamison
    B. Vince Carter
    C. Jason Williams
    D. Mike Bibby

22. Which player did Vancouver trade to San Antonio in exchange for Carl Herrera and the rights to Felipe Lopez?
    A. Doug Edwards
    B. Antonio Daniels
    C. Otis Thorpe
    D. Chris Robinson

Bonus Three-Pointers

23. Who was the first player ever signed by the Grizzlies?
A. Greg Antony
B. Kevin Pritchard
C. Ashraf Amaya
D. Chris Robinson

24. Which player's tip-in at the buzzer in OT gave Vancouver its first-ever win at home on November 5, 1995?
A. Antonio Harvey
B. Anthony Avent
C. Cuonzo Martin
D. Chris King

25. Name the Vancouver player who was invited to participate in the Long Distance Shootout at the 1998 NBA All-Star Weekend in New York.
A. Sam Mack
B. Pete Chilcutt
C. Anthony Peeler
D. Lee Mayberry

🎾 ANSWERS

1. C	10. C	19. C
2. B	11. A	20. B
3. A	12. B	21. D
4. D	13. C	22. B
5. B	14. A	23. B
6. C	15. A	24. D
7. C	16. D	25. A
8. D	17. C	
9. A	18. B	

WASHINGTON WIZARDS

Their nickname and arena may be new, but the Washington Wizards have a long and storied history in the NBA. Like the District of Columbia itself, this team is always full of surprises.

FREE THROWS

1. **Which player did Washington send to Sacramento in exchange for Mitch Richmond and Otis Thorpe on May 14, 1998?**
   A. Juwan Howard
   B. Rod Strickland
   C. Calbert Cheaney
   D. Chris Webber

2. **The Wizards now play at the MCI Center in downtown Washington. In which city did they previously play their home games?**
   A. Baltimore, Md.
   B. Landover, Md.
   C. Chevy Chase, Md.
   D. Annapolis, Md.

3. **Where did longtime Washington player and executive Wes Unseld attend college?**
   A. Kentucky
   B. UCLA
   C. Louisville
   D. Syracuse

TWO-POINTERS

4. **Which coach in Wizards franchise history twice won Coach of the Year honors?**
   A. Gene Shue
   B. Bernie Bickerstaff
   C. Dick Motta
   D. Kevin Loughery

5. **Which of the following players has *not* had his number retired by Washington?**
   A. Phil Chenier
   B. Elvin Hayes
   C. Gus Johnson
   D. Wes Unseld

6. **Which Washington player won the three-point shootout at the 1996 NBA All-Star Weekend?**
   A. Michael Adams
   B. Tim Legler
   C. Tracy Murray
   D. Brent Price

7. Before the Wizards moved to Washington, there was another team that called the city home. The Washington Capitols, however, only lasted five seasons in the league. But one of the most successful coaches in NBA history led the Capitols for three of their five seasons. Name the coach.
    A. Joe Lapchick
    B. Red Holzman
    C. Red Auerbach
    D. John Kundla

8. In which season did Washington win its only NBA title?
    A. 1971–72
    B. 1975–76
    C. 1977–78
    D. 1978–79

9. Who was the head coach of that championship team?
    A. Dick Motta
    B. Wes Unseld
    C. Mike Farmer
    D. Gene Shue

10. Name the Hall of Fame guard who began his career with the Baltimore Bullets but had his number retired by the Knicks.
    A. Walt Frazier
    B. Dick McGuire
    C. Dick Barnett
    D. Earl Monroe

11. Rod Strickland led the NBA in assists in 1997–98. Which other Washington player has led the league in that category?
    A. Brent Price
    B. Kevin Porter
    C. Michael Adams
    D. Archie Clark

12. **Which of the following Washington players did *not* win the NBA Most Improved Player award?**
    A. Pervis Ellison
    B. Michael Adams
    C. Gheorghe Muresan
    D. Don MacLean

13. **Name the only player other than Wilt Chamberlain in NBA history to win Rookie of the Year and MVP honors in the same season.**
    A. Wes Unseld
    B. Earl Monroe
    C. Walt Bellamy
    D. Bernard King

14. **Which three-time member of the All-NBA First Team is Washington's career leader in scoring and blocked shots?**
    A. Jeff Malone
    B. Gus Johnson
    C. Jack Marin
    D. Elvin Hayes

15. **Which of the following coaches never guided the Wizards?**
    A. K.C. Jones
    B. Pat Riley
    C. Jim Lynam
    D. Buddy Jeannette

16. **Who is Washington's all-time career leader in steals?**
    A. Greg Ballard
    B. Frank Johnson
    C. Phil Chenier
    D. Elvin Hayes

17. Name the 7'7" player from the University of Bridgeport whom Washington selected in the 1985 draft.
    A. Gheorghe Muresan
    B. Jim McIlvaine
    C. Manute Bol
    D. Alan Ogg

18. When Walt Bellamy won Rookie of the Year honors in 1962, where was the franchise located?
    A. Chicago
    B. Baltimore
    C. Washington
    D. Milwaukee

19. Which Washington player was the 1991 High School Player of the Year in Illinois?
    A. Calbert Cheaney
    B. Juwan Howard
    C. Rod Strickland
    D. Tracy Murray

20. Washington played the same team in its consecutive trips to the NBA Finals. Which team was it?
    A. Portland Trail Blazers
    B. Los Angeles Lakers
    C. Houston Rockets
    D. Seattle SuperSonics

21. The team was called the Bullets for 34 years before making a change to the Wizards. What was the first season that the club was known as the Wizards?
    A. 1994–95
    B. 1995–96
    C. 1996–97
    D. 1997–98

22. **Wizard Mitch Richmond is one of only four players in the NBA to have averaged 21-plus points in each of his first 10 professional seasons. Who doesn't belong in this elite group?**
    A. Oscar Robertson
    B. Kareem Abdul-Jabbar
    C. Larry Bird
    D. Michael Jordan

BONUS THREE-POINTERS

23. **1990 was the only year that three players who had played for the same franchise were inducted into the Hall of Fame. Who were they?**
    A. Wes Unseld, Phil Chenier, Earl Monroe
    B. Phil Chenier, Walt Bellamy, Bailey Howell
    C. Elvin Hayes, Gus Johnson, Walt Bellamy
    D. Elvin Hayes, Earl Monroe, Dave Bing

24. **The Washington Wizards franchise was born in Chicago as the Packers. What other nickname did the team go by before moving east to Baltimore/Washington?**
    A. Zephyrs
    B. Stags
    C. Rebels
    D. Falcons

25. **Which team did the Wizards beat 95–78 in the inaugural game at MCI Center?**
    A. Boston Celtics
    B. Seattle SuperSonics
    C. Charlotte Hornets
    D. San Antonio Spurs

❂ ANSWERS

1. D	14. D
2. B	15. B
3. C	16. A
4. A	17. C
5. A	18. A
6. B	19. B
7. C	20. A
8. C	21. A
9. A	22. C
10. D	23. D
11. B	24. A
12. B	25. B
13. A	

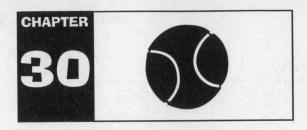

RULES OF THE GAME

While the game of basketball requires only a ball and a hoop, the NBA version is a little more complex. From the court to the locker room, the rules of the game can test even an expert.

FREE THROWS

1. **How high off the ground is the rim of an NBA basket?**
   - A. 8 feet
   - B. 10 feet
   - C. 12 feet
   - D. 15 feet

2. **What is the diameter of an official NBA basketball?**
   - A. 7 inches
   - B. 8 inches
   - C. 9 inches
   - D. 10 inches

3. **How long is a regulation period of an NBA game?**
   - A. 10 minutes
   - B. 12 minutes
   - C. 15 minutes
   - D. 20 minutes

TWO-POINTERS

4. **What is the minimum number of players an NBA team must have dressed in uniform and on the bench for a game?**
    A. 7
    B. 8
    C. 9
    D. 10

5. **What is the maximum distance of the three-point line from the basket in an NBA game?**
    A. 19 feet, 9 inches
    B. 21 feet
    C. 22 feet
    D. 23 feet, 9 inches

6. **How long is the overtime period of an NBA game?**
    A. Until the first team scores
    B. 5 minutes
    C. 10 minutes
    D. 15 minutes

7. **According to the rule book, who is allowed to speak to the referees during a timeout?**
    A. captain(s) only
    B. coaches only
    C. captains and coaches
    D. no one

8. **How much time does an offensive team have to move the ball over the midcourt line?**
    A. 5 seconds
    B. 10 seconds
    C. 15 seconds
    D. no limit

9. **How wide is an NBA foul lane?**
   A. 15 feet
   B. 16 feet
   C. 18 feet
   D. 20 feet

10. **How much pressure must there be in an NBA ball?**
    A. between 7 ½ and 8 ½ pounds
    B. between 8 and 9 pounds
    C. between 8 ½ and 9 ½ pounds
    D. no requirement

11. **What is the diameter of the NBA basket rim?**
    A. 14 inches
    B. 16 inches
    C. 18 inches
    D. 20 inches

12. **In which season did the NBA institute the 24-second shot clock?**
    A. 1946–47
    B. 1949–50
    C. 1952–53
    D. 1954–55

13. **A player attempting a free throw must do so within a specific amount of time after receiving the ball from the referee, or else he forfeits his attempt. How much time does a player have in which to shoot?**
    A. 5 seconds
    B. 10 seconds
    C. 15 seconds
    D. 20 seconds

14. When a player commits his sixth personal foul, he is disqualified from the game and must be replaced in the lineup. How long does a coach have to decide on a replacement?
    A. 30 seconds
    B. 60 seconds
    C. 2 minutes
    D. a "reasonable" amount of time

15. What is the standard amount of time between halves of an NBA game?
    A. 5 minutes
    B. 10 minutes
    C. 15 minutes
    D. 20 minutes

16. How many technical fouls result in ejection from the game?
    A. one
    B. two
    C. three
    D. four

17. How many assistant coaches are permitted to sit on the bench during a game?
    A. one
    B. two
    C. three
    D. four

18. What are the dimensions of an NBA backboard?
    A. 6 feet by 3 feet
    B. 6 feet by 3 ½ feet
    C. 6 feet by 4 feet
    D. 6 feet by 4 ½ feet

19. **How many assists can be awarded for a successful field goal?**
    A. one
    B. two
    C. three
    D. no limit

20. **How much time does a player have to inbound the ball?**
    A. 3 seconds
    B. 5 seconds
    C. 10 seconds
    D. 15 seconds

21. **According to the official rule book, what is the optimum size of an NBA court?**
    A. 50 feet by 94 feet
    B. 50 feet by 100 feet
    C. 54 feet by 94 feet
    D. 54 feet by 100 feet

22. **How many timeouts are each team allowed per game? (Do not include 20-second timeouts.)**
    A. 3
    B. 5
    C. 7
    D. 9

BONUS THREE-POINTERS

23. **Who invented the 24-second clock?**
    A. Maurice Podoloff
    B. Red Auerbach
    C. Walter Brown
    D. Danny Biasone

24. **In which season did the NBA start using three referees per game instead of only two?**
    A. 1988–89
    B. 1989–90
    C. 1990–91
    D. 1991–92

25. **How long does a team have to protest the outcome of a game?**
    A. 24 hours
    B. 48 hours
    C. one week
    D. two weeks

ANSWERS

1. B	14. A
2. C	15. C
3. B	16. B
4. B	17. C
5. D	18. B
6. B	19. A
7. A	20. B
8. B	21. A
9. B	22. C
10. A	23. D
11. C	24. A
12. D	25. B
13. B	